Creating Your Own
SUCCESS
COLLEGE STUDY SKILLS

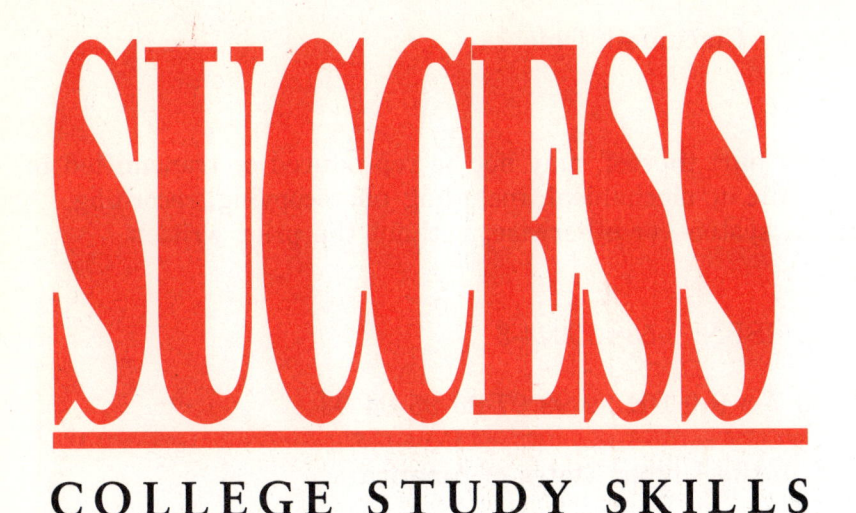

V. Rose Kitchen
Writer and Consultant

MaryAnn Moore
President, Wynmor Inc.

SOUTH-WESTERN PUBLISHING CO.

Copyright © 1994

by SOUTH-WESTERN PUBLISHING CO.

Cincinnati, Ohio

ALL RIGHTS RESERVED

The text of this publication, or any part thereof, may not be reproduced or transmitted in any form or by any means, electronic or mechanical, including photocopying, recording, storage in an information retrieval system, or otherwise, without the prior written permission of the publisher.

ISBN: 0-538-70924-3

1 2 3 4 5 6 7 8 9 0 DH 99 98 97 96 95 94 93

Printed in the United States of America

Managing/Acquisitions Editor:	Karen Schneiter
Developmental Editor:	Susan Freeman
Coordinating Editor:	Gayle Entrup
Production Manager:	Deborah Luebbe
Production Editor:	Edna D. Stroble
Senior Production Editor:	Jane Congdon
Senior Designer:	Jim DeSollar
Associate Photo Editor/Stylist:	Linda Ellis
Cover Photo:	Mark Keller/Superstock
Senior Marketing Manager:	Carolyn Love

Photo Credits:
- page 3   H. Armstrong Roberts
- page 142   Richard Younker
- page 146   George Bellerose/Stock, Boston
- page 185   Laimute E. Druskis/Stock, Boston

Library of Congress Cataloging-in-Publication Data

Kitchen, V. Rose, 1941-
　Creating your own success: college study skills / V. Rose Kitchen, MaryAnn Moore.
　　p.　cm.
　Includes index.
　ISBN 0-538-70924-3
　1. Study skills. 2. College student orientation.　I. Moore, MaryAnn, 1952- . II. Title.
LB2395.K38　　1994　　　　　　　　　　　93-30556
378.1'7028'12--dc20　　　　　　　　　　　CIP

This Book Is Dedicated To:

My mother, LEE ANN GOODPASTURE,
who taught me to be independent and curious.

MaryAnn Moore

and

All of the students who inspired me
to participate in the writing of this book.

V. Rose Kitchen

Thank You:

Linda Kistner
Deena Grace
Judy Paste
All of our former students
Reviewers

Nancy Browning, Lincoln University; Deborah Daiek, Wayne State University; Judy R. Heumann, Portland Community College; Charles Jones, Jr., Central Connecticut State University; Jane Kavanaugh, Vincennes University; Thomas Larimer, Southern Ohio College; Susan Martin, University of South Florida; Brenda Miller, North Iowa Area Community College; Sue Perry, Sawyer Business School; and Cynthia Turner, St. Phillip's College.

Christine Cabral, Dean of Students, Florida School of Business
James D. Monahan
Richard E. Kitchen

This Guide Is The Personal Property Of:

NAME

COURSE TITLE

CLASS HOUR

INSTRUCTOR

Daily affirmations for creating my own success:

A purpose to fill my days,
Goals to fill my mind.

My life will be a beautiful thing,
Filled with the joys success can bring.

My tomorrows will be better than the rest,
By giving of my best.

Giving 100% when faced with a task,
For my success this is not too much to ask.

To bring about all I wish to achieve,
In myself I must believe.

Contents

Introduction — ix

Chapter 1: **Getting Acquainted** — 1
- Why This Class Is Offered — 3
- How You Will Benefit from This Class — 4
- Getting Acquainted — 4
- The Purpose of This Student Guide — 5
- Chapter Overviews — 5
- Tips on Getting Acquainted — 7
- Campus Resources — 10

Chapter 2: **Goals** — 21
- Steps to Achieve Goals — 22
- Goal Busters — 22
- Three Types of Goals — 23
- You'll Never Make It — 28
- Enjoying Every Step — 28
- Talkers and Doers — 28
- Chance and Change — 29
- Visualize Success — 31

Chapter 3: **Listening** — 39
- Why Listening Is Important — 40
- Stumbling Blocks to Listening — 41
- Effective Listening Techniques — 42
- Exercise Your Listening — 44

Chapter 4: Reading and Taking Notes — 55

- Reading — 56
- Types of Reading — 57
- Preparing Mentally for Effective Reading — 58
- Notes — 61
- Taking Notes — 62

Chapter 5: Attitudes — 73

- Attitudes — 74
- Understanding Attitudes — 74
- Turning Your Attitudes Around — 76
- Guidelines in Human Relations — 77
- Freckles or Warts — 79
- Your Mind and Your Attitude — 80
- Changing for the Better — 82

Chapter 6: Time Management — 95

- Basic Time Management Principles — 96
- Time-Management Tools — 102

Chapter 7: Memory Techniques — 123

- Long- and Short-term Memory — 124
- Condition Yourself to Remember — 124
- Attention and Concentration Are Important — 125
- Memory Techniques to Use All your Senses — 125
- Organize What You Are Trying to Remember — 126
- Be Repetitive — 127
- Be Creative — 128
- Try Clustering — 129

Chapter 8	**Test-Taking Techniques**	**141**
	Prepare Mentally for Test Taking	142
	Develop a Test-Taking Strategy	146
	How to Handle Specific Question Types	147
	Who Gets Cheated?	151
Chapter 9	**Body Language and Appearance**	**161**
	Body Language	162
	Appearance	165
Chapter 10	**Drug and Alcohol Abuse**	**179**
	A Hundred and One Reasons	181
	Learning to Say No	182
	How Do I Know If It's Use or Abuse?	187
	Toward Recovery	188
Chapter 11	**Relationships**	**199**
	Communication	200
	Change	203
	Appreciation	204
	Relationships That Hurt: Being Battered	205
	Sexual Harassment	206
Chapter 12	**Burnout and Self-Motivation**	**217**
	Burnout	218
	Self-Motivation	221
	A Few of the Secrets of Life	225
	Index	**239**

Introduction

Congratulations! You have just started a learning adventure that will change your life. The thought of starting college was probably exciting but also a little scary. Don't worry if you have some doubts about your success; this is natural. All of us have a tendency to wonder at the start of a new project if we will do well . This book will help you by covering the special skills needed to reach your goal of graduation. Your college administrators have included this textbook in your course of study because they care about you and want you to succeed. During this course you will be refreshed in the basic skills of effective listening, remembering information, reading for content, note taking, and test-taking techniques. In addition, lectures, class discussions, and exercises will help you learn a great deal about yourself and others. The subjects of goal setting, body language, appearance, drug and alcohol abuse, relationships, burnout, attitudes, time management, and self-motivation will help you deal with life effectively. By learning to solve the daily problems that come up in life, you will greatly increase your chances for success.

Now that you know why you are taking this class, let's learn more about the book. The writing style has been kept simple and direct so you can understand and use the information right away. You will find not only student exercises but also case studies which will help you explore new ways of thinking. At the end of Chapter 12, you will find pages on which to write or attach motivational sayings. It will help you keep a successful attitude if you start collecting these sayings and look at them often. You may even want to set up motivational saying exchanges in which you share the sayings which help motivate you with classmates and learn their favorites. Most of the exercises and case studies can be completed during class, so classroom participation is important. Besides, you'll learn more and have more fun if you make friends right away. To help you do this, your first chapter is called "Getting Acquainted." At the end of each chapter is a list of additional resources where you can find more information about the subject you just studied. Most of these books should be available in your local library or through bookstores.

How did this book get the title *Creating Your Own Success*? Since the book was developed specifically to help empower you to reach goals that in the past were only dreams, each word was chosen carefully. As you complete the various chapters, you will see that you are developing "how to" skills and the positive self-awareness necessary to CREATE success in your studies. Renewed self-confidence and self-esteem will allow you to begin focusing on

SUCCESS rather than failure. Small successes will build into big successes, and soon you will notice changes in how you think and feel about the events in your life. Probably the most important words in the title are YOUR OWN, for no one can do this for you. This book will guide, your instructor will help, your classmates will encourage, but only you have the power to make the changes that you desire.

In this book you will find no tests to be taken, no massive amounts of reading, but instead a simple guide to success — a personal record of experiences and methods yet to be experienced by you that will become a self-reference of who you are today and who you plan to be tomorrow. Exercises, case studies for group discussion, and sheets for personal comments at the front of each chapter will help you strengthen your understanding of the material. At the end of this course, by filling out the five self-positives at the beginning of every chapter you will have defined sixty qualities you like about yourself. The personal comment sheet, in addition to having a space for five self-positives, also has a self-affirming statement. The "Getting Focused" section at the bottom of the sheet helps you think about how the chapter will help you reach your goal. By the time you finish this book, you will be well prepared for the challenges and opportunities of your future.

You have already taken the hardest step toward success by starting school. The college staff, your instructors, the new friends you will make, and this guide will be there to help you. You are no longer alone in your struggle for success and a better life. By concentrating on attitude and attendance, you will be picking up your diploma and interviewing for jobs before you know it. Once again, congratulations on your decision to start school. You should be very proud.

Now a Few Words about Attendance

It is important! You must decide today that you are going to attend all of your classes every day if humanly possible. The greatest college instructors in the world can't help you if you are not in class. You may think you already understand the information in your textbooks, but attending class will give you the opportunity to lock the knowledge deeper into your memory. This concept will be discussed further in Chapter 7. Also, by attending class you will have an opportunity to ask questions and learn additional information not covered in your textbooks.

A good way to motivate yourself out of bed in the morning is to remember that you are paying for the classes you will miss and not getting anything in return. Each and every time you choose to miss a class it is the same as throwing money in the trash.

Chapter 1

Getting Acquainted

"Today I will add one new friend to add to my success network"

Personal Comment Sheet

Entry Date

Five self-positives:

1.

2.

3.

4.

5.

Getting Focused

How do I think the information I am about to read will help me reach my goals?

Chapter 1

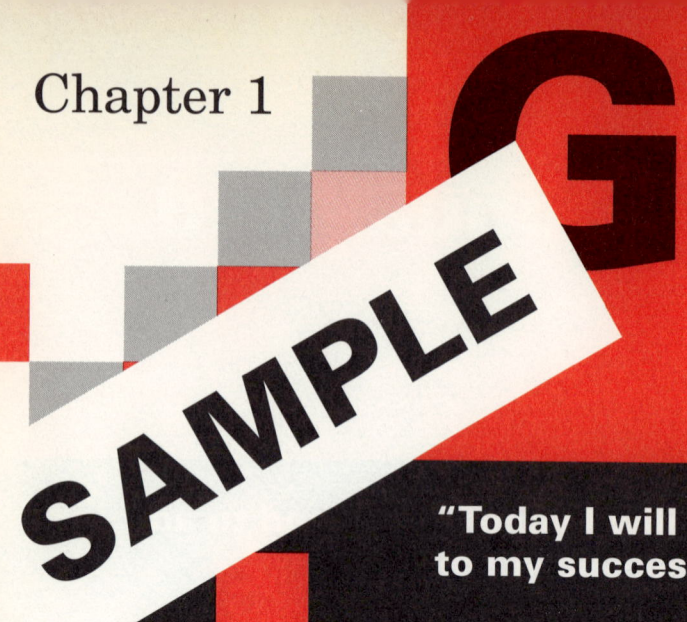

Getting Acquainted

"Today I will add one new friend to add to my success network"

Personal Comment Sheet

Entry Date **2.12.93**

Five self-positives:

1. **I am a good listener.**
2. **I have a great sense of humor.**
3. **I never quit.**
4. **I am enthusiastic.**
5. **I am determined.**

Getting Focused

How do I think the information I am about to read will help me reach my goals?
Feeling confident in my ability to make new acquaintances will be an asset to future career opportunities. Sometimes who you know really counts.
I met my new classmates this week and they were just as nervous as I was about meeting people. The hardest thing was standing up in front of the class and introducing myself.

Figure 1-1

Meeting new friends makes for a strong network.

H. Armstrong Roberts

Congratulations! You are about to join the ranks of hundreds of other students who have been where you are right now. These successful students have already tried and tested the techniques in this guide and have proven that they work. Learning is an ongoing process, and acquiring the valuable learning techniques in this book will make the process easier and more enjoyable.

How you begin the process is very important; therefore the first classes are devoted to getting acquainted with the instructor, classmates, and this student guide.

Why This Class Is Offered

You've always wanted to fly. For years it's been your only dream. As you stand at the edge of a runway, I walk up behind you and hand you the keys to my Lear Jet. Your mouth drops open in surprise as the keys glitter in your hand. At last, opportunity has knocked! But as you slip into the pilot's seat, you look at all the gauges, levers, and controls and realize you don't know what you are doing. Opportunity has knocked, but you're not ready. In that cockpit, faced with the reality of what it means to fly, you see your dream begin to slip through your hands. But wait, you are not a quitter! So slowly you build up your courage and ask me to teach you the things you need to know to reach your dream. Opportunity has knocked, and though you are not quite ready, you are ready to learn. And that is why this class is offered.

You too are reaching for a dream by starting school. And the very fact that you are here means that opportunity has knocked. Your time is now. Though the classes, textbooks, and instructors you're faced with may seem just as overwhelming as the gauges in our fictional cockpit, all you have to do is turn the pages of this book. Inside you will find information on attitudes, goal setting, relationships, and self-motivation. You will learn to sharpen your test-taking, note-taking, reading, and listening skills. You will

Chapter 1   **Getting Acquainted**

develop friendships and build a strong success network. After graduation, when an employer sees that you possess both the human skills and knowledge for the job he will hand you the "keys" without hesitation. Opportunity has knocked, and we are going to open the door together.

How You Will Benefit from This Class

This book and your instructor will help you strengthen your study skills and habits. By reading and using the information that will be covered in this class you will notice positive personal change.

Study Benefits

You will find that you can retrieve facts quicker and calm your nerves before a test. Listening more effectively and using your time wisely will become new good habits. As you read your textbooks, you will find it easier to understand the information, and taking notes will become second nature.

Change and Communication

We will start by helping you get to know your classmates and instructor. The next step will be to build a positive success network so that you share the strength of others as you stretch to reach your goal. You will learn how your attitude and those of others affect the chance for success. Both setting and reaching goals will be covered and you will be given many opportunities to practice these positive skills. You will learn to evaluate relationships, and understand nonverbal communication and the importance of first impressions. Drug and alcohol abuse and stress and burnout will be covered so that you do not get sidetracked on your road to success. Before you leave this class we will be sharing with you how you can keep yourself motivated on a daily basis. Yes, by the time this class ends, with a little work on your part, you will be ready to fly!

Getting Acquainted

Begin your success networking from the start by becoming acquainted with your instructor, classmates, and this student guide.

Instructor

By listening, watching, and asking questions, you will learn more from your instructor. The instructor will be the head of your success network and will supply you with the knowledge you need to create your own success. Your instructor was once a student and can help you to understand that getting an education is just the first step of many you will take in life.

Classmates

Don't be afraid to introduce yourself and talk with your classmates. You may be surprised at how different their backgrounds are. Regardless of backgrounds, you all have one thing in common — the desire *to be a success.* One of the most valuable techniques you can acquire is the ability to learn from other people's experiences.

Student Guide

Scan through this book — just get acquainted with *Creating Your Own Success.*

The Purpose of This Student Guide

This student guide is more than just a workbook. It is meant to be a source of reference for your entire academic experience.

Personal Comment Pages

The personal comment pages are diary pages where you can record your personal comments, five personal positives, and get focused on how this information will benefit you before you begin each chapter. As with each detail in this book, there is a reason the personal comment page starts off every chapter.

You have just spent two hours on math and one on English when you remember you have to read a chapter in this book. You feel overwhelmed. Disgusted. Or just plain worn out. But since you take reaching your goal seriously, you open the book. The first thing you are asked to do is write down five things you like about yourself. As you look at the good qualities you just listed, you find a smile creeping up. And suddenly you feel powerful and ready to tackle something new. Next you write a brief statement about how you feel the information you are about to read will help you reach your goals. Now you feel good about yourself and you are focused. Congratulations! You have just learned one of the secrets to self-motivation. When you start something new, concentrate on the positive, focus on how this experience can help you reach your goals, and above all — keep going.

Chapter Exercises and Case Studies

The chapter exercises and case studies are reinforcement for the lectures and will help you to practice what you are learning. The chapters contain written information to help lock in the more difficult subjects.

The student exercises, case studies, and notes are to be used in classroom discussions. For this purpose you must keep your assignments current.

Chapter Overviews

Let's take a quick look at the content of each of the lecture chapters.

Chapter 1   **Getting Acquainted**   **5**

Chapter 1 — Getting Acquainted

This chapter will help you and your classmates get to know each other. Chapter 1 contains information on your student guide and suggested ice breakers.

Chapter 2 — Goals

Goal setting is important to achieve success. This chapter contains ideas and methods you can use in setting and obtaining your goals, and student exercises and case studies to help you not only hear the information but think about it, say it, see it, and write it, putting as many of your five senses to work as possible. You will also find suggested resource materials — to help bring the importance of goals into focus.

Chapter 3 — Listening

This chapter covers techniques to help you listen more effectively. The chapter explains listening as one of the five senses and why it is important to develop all the senses for maximum learning ability. Barriers to effective listening and ways to overcome them are covered. Listening exercises and case studies help you determine what your listening barriers are and which of the techniques you can use to break them down.

Chapter 4 — Reading and Taking Notes

Since so much of your time is spent reading, the information in this chapter shows you how to pick out the important information as you read. It explains how to take usable notes, provides a student exercise on making a list of ways you can develop your reading ability, and gives examples to help you create your own note-taking styles.

Chapter 5 — Attitudes

How success is affected by the proper attitude is explained in this chapter. Proven methods you can use to develop good attitudes and how bad attitudes are usually acquired are discussed. An attitude-awareness exercise asks you to look at your attitude toward people and circumstances in your life and ways you can improve your attitude.

Chapter 6 — Time Management

After a few weeks of classes and homework, you may begin to feel time pressures. The time-management techniques in this chapter will help you to see the importance of using your time wisely. Student exercises will show you exactly how you are using your time and how many hours a week you actually have to spend on schoolwork.

Chapter 7 — Memory Techniques

This chapter describes the different types of memory and things that can hamper recall. Memory techniques and exercises are included, once again using the five senses to help in the development of good memory recall.

Chapter 8 — Test-Taking Techniques

This chapter starts with ways to overcome the fear of tests. It explains the different types of tests and includes tips on studying for tests and how to take them. At the end of Chapter 8 you will actually help develop a "mock" test with your classmates.

Chapter 9 — Body Language and Appearance

How body language is used to communicate nonverbal messages is covered here. Also discussed are the types of messages communicated through body language, both consciously and unconsciously. Establishing the right kind of image through appearance is discussed. Exercises and case studies give you a chance to practice positive nonverbal communication and help you start to develop a wardrobe inventory.

Chapter 10 — Drug and Alcohol Abuse

This important chapter gives general information about the harmful effects that drugs and alcohol have on human lives. Information on drug testing and suggestions for getting outside help are included.

Chapter 11 — Relationships

The three elements involved in maintaining successful relationships — communication, change, and appreciation — are covered in this chapter. Guidelines that can help you cope with these three elements are discussed. So that your relationships are rich in variety, cultural diversity and the benefits of friendships with people from differing backgrounds will be discussed. In addition, you will learn to recognize and deal with sexual harassment.

Chapter 12 — Burnout and Self-Motivation

The reasons some students experience burnout are covered in the last chapter. The traps they fall into trying to use short-term, quick fixes, and ways to handle burnout are discussed. Tips for self-motivation and how to spot the demotivators are also covered.

Tips on Getting Acquainted

Being able to meet people easily is a skill you can learn. It is a very important skill because it will help you succeed in all areas of life. Practice the following tips on your classmates and enjoy the new friendships you will make.

What's Your Name?

Remember that a person's name is very important to him or her. Make sure you get it right and use it during the conversation.

Look the Other Person in the Eyes

In many cultures, good eye contact makes people feel more comfortable with you. Using your eyes effectively will help you establish a bond with the other person. An additional benefit of good eye contact is that it will help you see whether the person understands and/or agrees with what you are saying. As you practice good eye contact, remember to respect the other person's cultural background. A good rule of thumb is not to exceed the level of eye contact that they display. Also keep in mind that staring makes people uncomfortable and should be avoided.

Figure 1-2

Good eye contact helps establish a bond with another person.

Ask Questions

A good way to get to know people is to ask questions that require more than a yes or no answer. For example, if you ask your new classmate, Mariesha, if she likes baseball she can answer with a simple yes or no. If you ask her what her favorite sport is she will have to give you a longer answer that will then lead to more questions or comments.

Focus on the Other Person

Remember, most people like to talk about themselves, so this is always a good place to start a conversation. Rather than beginning a conversation with the general request "Tell me about yourself," give the person a specific place to start by asking about jobs, children, hobbies, or pets. This is a particularly effective technique for those of us that feel shy in new situations.

Listen

A good conversationalist learns that one of the secrets is to listen more than you talk. After all, if you spend most of the time talking, you won't learn anything new from the other person. Remember that when listening to other people you should ask yourself what their words mean to them. Learn to listen from their perspective. Then take time to think before you speak.

Don't Interrupt

Allow the other person to complete each sentence before you begin to talk. It is bad manners to speak in the middle of another person's sentence.

Look for Common Interest

Try to find something that you have in common with the other person and start your conversation there. For example, all of you are students and have decided to start a new career. Learn why classmates chose their program of study or what motivated them to start school now.

You Don't Have to Be Shy

If you think of yourself as shy and have difficulty meeting people, realize that it is within your power to change. Being comfortable meeting people is a skill you can learn, and school is a great place to practice. When you meet a new person, rather than focusing on the discomfort you feel, concentrate on learning one interesting thing about this person. When you read Chapter 2 make this change one of your goals.

Be Enthusiastic

Be animated and show energy when you talk. Your enthusiasm will draw people to you.

Smile

Approximately 75% of our nonverbal communication is done with our faces. Smile when you meet someone new and show him/her through your facial expressions that you are enjoying the experience.

Speak Up

Remember that how you say something is just as important as what you say. Practice speaking clearly and loudly enough so that you can be understood and heard.

Practice Good Posture

When you talk, stand or sit up straight. Your posture is one of the first things other people notice about you. Keep your head up so that you can look at the other person and practice good eye contact.

Concentrate on Your Conversation

Learn not to be distracted by other people or the activities around you. Instead, make the other person feel important by focusing directly on him or her.

Eliminate Fillers

Tape your voice and get rid of filler words or phrases; for example: *like, um, you know*. Instead of using these fillers, substitute a breath.

Build Your Network

Remember that most of your classmates are just as nervous as you are, though they may show it differently. There is no reason to be afraid of them. Instead, enrich your life by adding them to your success network of positive people who will support your desire to complete school.

Campus Resources

It is important that you get acquainted with the offices, organizations and support personnel on campus. When you need assistance, knowing where to find it quickly can help you reach your goals. Take time now to find out the names of the support people at your school. The following resources can be found on most campuses; however, the office names may vary.

School Catalog or Bulletin

The school catalog or bulletin can be one of your most important resources. It contains information on class requirements, graduation requirements, admissions, financial aid, academics, student services, placement assistance, maps and layout of the campus, the academic calendar, and much more.

Student Services

Student Services can help you with counseling needs, both personal and academic. If the people in this office are unable to give you assistance, they will try to help you find organizations or agencies equipped to handle your particular need. Usually they can also give you information on transportation and car pooling.

Academic Dean/Registrar

If you need assistance with transferring credits, a change of major, transcripts, or adding or dropping classes, this is the office to visit.

Financial Aid

Financial Aid can answer your questions concerning the different types of financial assistance available and explain the paperwork involved.

School Organizations

School organizations can be valuable not only as a source of information, but for entertainment and friendship. Make a list of student clubs and groups that interest you.

Employment Assistance

The Employment Services department is where you will find information on part-time employment and career placement after graduation.

Tutoring

Tutoring is usually available through academic advisers or student services. Remember to talk to your instructor right away if you are having problems.

Other On-Campus Resources

Some other on-campus resources you will want to investigate are the library, health care facilities, available parking, and break rooms or cafeterias.

My Resource List

- Have I read the entire college catalog?   Yes   No

- If I need personal or academic counseling, I should see:

  Name

  Phone   Location

- If I need a schedule change or to transfer a class, I should make an appointment with:

  Name

  Phone   Location

- My Financial Aid adviser is:

  Name

  Phone   Location

- List school organizations, placing a check mark next to the ones that interest me most.

  _____   _____

  _____   _____

  _____   _____

  _____   _____

- Before I graduate I will need to meet with:

  Name

  Phone   Location

  for employment assistance.

- If I have trouble in a class I should talk with:

  Name

  Phone   Location

  to get help.

- My adviser's name is:

  Name

  Phone   Location

Creating Your Own Success

● Other support people I should know:

_____
_____
_____
_____
_____
_____
_____
_____

Chapter 1

More Steps On My Road To Success
A Personal Review

1. What were the key concepts discussed about getting acquainted?

2. How do I plan to put my new getting acquainted knowledge into effect?

3. What are the areas I don't understand or need more information on?

4. What is my game plan for getting the additional information I need?

5. What positive changes do I see in myself?

Chapter 1 Getting Acquainted

Exercise 1

You're the Master of Ceremonies

Getting to know your classmates as quickly as possible will help you by making you part of a success-oriented team. The purpose of this exercise is to allow you to get to know more about your classmates.

For the next five minutes, meet with the person your instructor matches you with and learn as much as possible about each other so that at the end of the time limit you can give your new friend a glowing introduction. Remember to include at least two interesting facts and one thing that you liked about them. Space has been left to enter this information. As the other people in your class are introduced, use the space following this assignment to mark down their names and information.

My New Friend's Name: _____

Program of Study: _____

Interesting Details: _____
_____

What I Liked: _____
_____

My Classmates:

Names	Program	How I Will Remember Them
_____	_____	_____
_____	_____	_____
_____	_____	_____
_____	_____	_____
_____	_____	_____
_____	_____	_____
_____	_____	_____
_____	_____	_____

Continue on separate sheet.

Chapter 1   Getting Acquainted

Exercise 2

My Life Sculpture

Your instructor is going to hand you two pipe cleaners and like an artist you are going to be given five minutes to shape one pipe cleaner to represent your life before today and the second one to represent the life you plan to have after graduation. At the end of the time limit your instructor will call on you to share the meaning of your "art."

Chapter 1 Getting Acquainted

Exercise 3

Some Important Things to Remember

About my class:

About my instructor:

About my classmates:

Chapter 1   Getting Acquainted

Case Study

Shy Anna

Anna has always been told by her parents that she is shy. As she goes in to meet with Mr. Sampson, the Academic Dean, her heart begins to beat fast, her palms start to sweat, and after a quick glance at him, her eyes stay focused on the floor. When she shakes his hand she does so with a limp grip and her voice is so soft that it can barely be heard above the office noise.

1. After this terrible meeting she rushes to your apartment and asks you, her best friend, for help. What do you suggest she do and how should she go about making the changes you suggest?

2. If you are like Anna, what do you intend to do to change? Remember during the group discussion to take notes on your classmates' ideas, putting stars next to the ones you plan to try first.

Creating Your Own Success

Suggested Resource Material

Books: Additional Resources

Carnegie, Dale, & Carnegie, Dorothy. *How to Win Friends and Influence People*. Simon & Schuster Publishing Co., 1981.

Martin, Judith. *Miss Manners*. Warner Books Publishing Co., 1988.

Baldridge, Letitia. *The Amy Vanderbilt Complete Book of Etiquette*. Doubleday Publishing Co., 1978.

Chapter 2
Goals

"I will review my goals vividly three times a day."

Personal Comment Sheet

Entry Date

Five self-positives:

1.

2.

3.

4.

5.

Getting Focused

How do I think the information I am about to read will help me reach my goals?

Goals are the difference between the desire to be and the determination to be. They are the foundation for every successful life because they take a dream and turn it into a plan of action. Without goals you do not have a clear picture in your mind of what you want and how you are going to get it. As you work through this chapter, keep in mind that your goals should be specific and measurable. For example, a goal of becoming a better person is too vague and cannot be measured. But rewritten as "I will become a better person by spending a minimum of three hours a week as a volunteer at the homeless shelter" meets the guidelines. It is both specific (you are going to spend at least three hours) and measurable (it is easy to see at the end of the week whether you put in the time).

Steps to Achieve Goals

Before you begin to actually write out your goals, it is important to understand the steps in goal setting.

1. Write out your goals.
2. Make a separate list showing the benefits of achieving each one of your goals.
3. List any problems that might make it difficult to achieve your goals and how you will overcome these roadblocks.
4. List your target date for reaching each of your goals. Make these target dates both challenging and realistic. Nothing is more discouraging than setting a goal you cannot possibly meet; for example: "I will lose a hundred pounds in two weeks."
5. Post your goals and positive statements you want to achieve where you will see them at least three times a day.

Goal Busters

Following the steps to goal setting will go a long way toward making sure that you are successful. But as added assurance so you don't get tripped up by goal busters, here's a list of problem areas to look out for:

- Vague goals
- Lack of discipline
- Spending too much time on friends, TV, or partying
- An "I don't care" attitude that is really just a cover-up for fear of failure
- Poor self-image
- Poor attendance
- Giving up when things get a little tough
- Believing people who say you can't make it

Figure 2-1

Your self-image is important to your goals.

Now is the best time to spot and stop any of these goal-buster qualities. If in reading this list, you wondered when and where the authors met you, it is a good bet you need to work to rid yourself of your personal goal-buster habits. Remember, only you can make your dreams turn into reality. And on the other side of that coin, only you can prevent it.

Three Types of Goals

Some goals take more thought, planning, and time to achieve than others. Your goals can be divided into three categories based on when you plan to reach them. These three categories are long-term, intermediate, and short-term. You can think of these three types of goals as steps on a ladder. Your short-term goals are the first rung on the ladder. To reach your intermediate goals, you have to take this first step. To make it to your long-term goals, you need to step on the intermediate rung. By taking each step in order and making sure they all work together, you can reach the top.

Long-Term Goals

First we will examine long-term goals. Long-term goals are those major accomplishments you wish to achieve in your lifetime. For example, look at the long-term goal categories in the following list:

- Education — Do you want to complete your education with a diploma, a certificate, or a degree?

- Career — What would you like to be doing at the time you retire?

- Self-worth — Would you feel better about yourself if you enhanced your appearance, increased your self-confidence, or improved your personal habits?

- Relationships — What type of relationships do you want? Friends? Co-workers? Family? Spouse?

- Home — Where do you want to live after you achieve career success? Where do you want to live after you retire? What type of house do you want?

- Finances — At what age do you want to be able to retire? What standard of living do you want?

- Travel — Where do you want to travel? How often?

Use Goal Sheet 1 on page 33 to make a list of your long-term goals. An example of a long-term goal would be "to earn an associate degree in fashion merchandising." Another might be "to work as the head buyer of children's clothing for a major department store."

Examine your long-term goals to see that they do not conflict. For example, if one long-term goal is to travel for six months every year and another is to own and manage a small day-care center, you may find it difficult to achieve both goals. Since most day-care owner/operators put in long hours, they do not have time for trips of this length.

After completing your list, look it over carefully and mark two goals you believe are the most important. Remember that one fundamental of goal achievement is the need to set a deadline for each goal. Make sure your deadline is realistic, but above all give yourself a specific date to aim for.

Once you have chosen your goals, you should identify specific steps that will help you achieve those goals. See the example in Figure 2-2.

Long-Term Goals — Life Achievements

Goal		To earn an associate degree in fashion merchandising
Deadline		Five years from today
Steps	1.	Get college catalog
	2.	Find money for tuition – check with financial aid office
	3.	Enroll and start classes within three months
	4.	
Goal		To work as the head buyer of children's clothing for a major department store
Deadline		In 2010
Steps	1.	Work as a sales clerk while working on degree
	2.	Apply for position as an assistant buyer after I earn degree
	3.	Work toward promotions
	4.	Work as a buyer for a small clothing store

Table 2-1
Long-Term Goals

Intermediate Goals

Intermediate goals are those you hope to reach in the next one to five years. For the person wanting an associate degree in fashion merchandising, an intermediate goal might be "to successfully complete two night classes each term to work toward my degree."

Use Goal Sheet 2 on page 34 to list your intermediate goals. After you have completed this list, go over it carefully and make sure your intermediate goals will help you achieve your long-term goals.

Short-Term Goals

Short-term goals are of particular importance for several reasons. First, a short-term goal that can be reached quickly allows you to experience how good it feels to reach a goal. This positive feeling helps increase your self-confidence and motivates you to continue reaching for your goals. In addition, long-term and intermediate goals are reached in little steps. These steps are known as short-

Chapter 2   Goals

Intermediate Goals — Next One to Five Years

Goal _Raise my grade point average to a 3.0_
Deadline _One and a half years_
Steps
1. _Study three hours a night_
2. _Spend two hours each Saturday at the library_
3. _Line up a tutor for English classes_
4. _____

Table 2-2

Intermediate Goals

term goals. For example, one of your goals is to graduate from school and get a good job. But this intermediate goal cannot be reached without a lot of short-term goals while you are in school; for example, passing your first test, getting a B or above on your first paper, making the honor roll by your second term. So remember — short-term, specific, measurable goals are the foundation for long-term success.

Short-term goals are the goals you plan to reach in less than a year. Again, your short-term goals should lead to the accomplishment of your intermediate and long-term goals. Short-term goals should be specific and require immediate action.

Figure 2-2

A short-term goal might be to spend five hours each week on homework for this class.

To use the person from the previous example, a short-term goal might be "to earn an A in business communication." A step toward this might be "to spend one hour five nights a week on homework and study for this class."

Use Goal Sheet 3 on page 35 to list your short-term goals.

Goal Action Plan

Once you have identified your goals, set deadlines, and listed steps, you can be sure of success — right? Not quite. Now comes the hard part. You must keep your commitment to your goals alive.

Right now you're probably pretty fired up about reaching your goals. They are new and fresh in your mind. But how do you keep them that way? Start by going over your goal sheets daily to see if you are doing the tasks necessary to attain them. Review your

Short-Term Goals — Specific in the Next Year

Goal   _To earn an A in business communications_

Deadline _This semester_

Steps 1. _Spend 1 hr. 5 nights a week on homework and study for this class_
2. _Attend all of Mr. Whitman's after-class sessions_
3. _Meet with my Success Network one week before all major projects are due in order to get feedback on my work_

Table 2-3

Short-Term Goals

goal sheets at least once a month with your new success network. During this meeting, discuss as a group what goals you have reached and which ones you are actively working on. And, before you end the meeting, don't forget to give yourself and others a big pat on the back for every step you have taken toward your goals.

What is another way you can make your goals come alive? Use a large poster board or note board suitable for framing and hang this board in a place at home that will be visible. See the example in Figure 2-6. Be creative and have fun! The board will be a constant reminder of your goals and your progress toward those goals. You can put any picture you choose on the board that represents your goals. When you have obtained one of the goals, you should mark your goal picture with a little flag, star, or whatever symbol you choose to signify that you have accomplished that goal.

Figure 2-3

Sample Goal Board

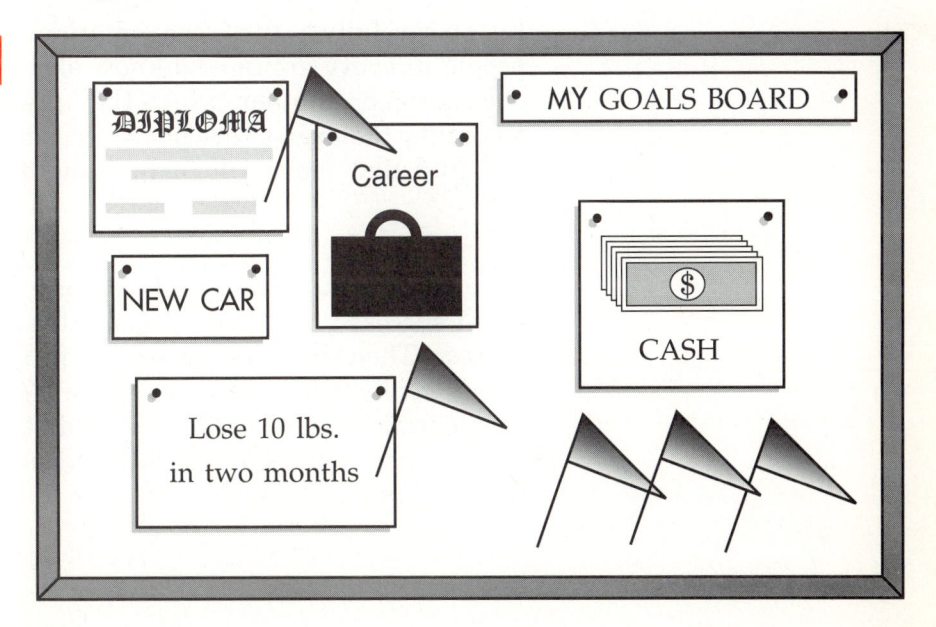

Chapter 2   Goals   27

You'll Never Make It

If these words sound familiar, you know what happens when you share your goals with "negative" people. It's a sad but true fact that not everyone will be supportive of your desire to improve yourself. Some of these people may be very dear to you. Others may be more easily laughed off. But however you react to their comments, the important thing is that you refuse to give them the power to shatter your dreams. Instead, think of their doubts as a dare. And then prove them wrong.

Enjoying Every Step

When you reach a goal it feels terrific. However, since we spend a lot more time working toward our goals than we do basking in the end result, we need to get pleasure during the process and not just at the end. That is why during your monthly success network goal check meetings it is important to give yourself pats on the back for each little step toward your goals.

But what if you have already caught yourself saying "I'll be happy when I reach Goal #1," or "My life will be great when I have finally lost weight, graduated, or am making $20,000.00 a year"? Stop and remind yourself that you are not going to put happiness on hold. Instead, replace those negative messages with ones that will help you enjoy the entire goal process. Try saying "I am happy because I am taking positive control of my life," or "I get pleasure from both the little steps and big leaps I take toward my goal."

Talkers and Doers

As a goal-oriented person, you will often find yourself in the company of other people who like to talk about success. There is a big difference between talking about success and putting in the effort to become successful.

Don't Hide Behind an Excuse

Listen carefully to these conversations and you will find one or two people in every group who know all the right techniques, but for one reason or another (which they are always eager to share with you), they themselves are not successful. As you listen to them, you will find that most will fit into one of these three categories:

"If only"

People who use the "if only" excuse will talk very persuasively about success until they are given the choice to work at their own success. Then their story goes "My grades would have been higher *if only* my instructor was better," or *"If only* there weren't so many people in this class," or *"If only* I didn't have to try and study when the kids are home." The "if only's" think it is never their fault that they are not successful.

"I couldda"

The "I couldda" group are the people who spend a lot of time talking about the past. *"I couldda* been more industrious with my studies." *"I couldda* listened closer and set my priorities." *"I couldda* practiced self-discipline." They are sure they "couldda" if only they "wouldda."

"I'm agonna"

The "I'm agonna" bunch are the men and women who think they want to succeed. They start out great, but just seem to run out of steam. They research all of the proven ways to be a success but get sidetracked easily. "Well sure, *I'm agonna* read that chapter in history — as soon as I get back from the mall." *"I'm agonna* get to class on time if my alarm clock doesn't make me late." *"I'm agonna* turn in my homework just as soon as I can find where the dog hid it." The "I'm agonna's" see themselves as they believe they are or want to be while others see them differently.

Be A "Plan-and-Do"

The truly successful people choose the "Plan-and-Do" technique. Of course the "I couldda's," "If only's," and the "I'm agonna's" think the "Plan-and-Do's" succeed because they just have a lot of luck.

The "Plan-and-Do's" finish what they start by taking the necessary steps needed to finish. "Plan-and-Do's" know that the secret to creating your own success depends on practicing self-discipline, showing enthusiasm, and being action motivated. "Plan-and-Do's" have an old saying they use as their motto: Plan your work, and work your plan. In watching "Plan-and-Do" people, it is easy to see why they reach their goals. They make their goals a number-one priority, work hard and smart, believe in themselves, and are willing to take well thought out risks.

Chance and Change

Be aware that when you set goals you are taking a chance. Taking a chance implies risk and most of us have not been taught to feel comfortable with risk taking. When you first enrolled for school, you may have worried about whether you could succeed or not. Goal setting can help insure success when you make a change (take a risk) in your life. Change is necessary for growth.

Look at how you react to change. Most of us would see winning a million dollars as positive. But wouldn't it also mean you would have to pay taxes on it, invest some of it so you would have money in the future, and begin wondering if any of your new friends liked you just for your money? This example shows that positive change has some negative aspects, just as negative events always have some positive aspects if we look for them. Can you think of examples from your life that show both the positive and negative sides of an event?

Facing the Unknown

Chances are, your first day of school you didn't know most of your instructors. The students that sat around you in class were strangers. You may have felt alone and uncomfortable. But you faced the unknown and now find yourself laughing about how "scared" you were that first day. What was just described is a normal reaction to change.

Every time we experience change, we also have to deal with the unknown. They go hand in hand. So it is important that we understand these feelings and also understand how not to let them overwhelm us.

The best way to combat feelings of discomfort during times of change is to get busy. If you find yourself feeling fearful or worrying about whether you will reach your goal, grab your action plan and get to work. For example, one of your goals is to get a C or above in all of your classes. But you are really having a tough time in English. Instead of sitting around complaining about what a lousy class English is, use your time to form a study group. Goal-oriented action like this will keep your mind busy in productive ways and not give you time to worry.

But I Can't Help Myself

If you still find that you have a hard time keeping the worry monster off your back, post the following information where you can see it. A University of Michigan study found that our fears can be broken down into the following general categories: totally unwarranted; have already taken place; too petty to bother with;

Figure 2-4

How Does My Success Grow?

How does my success grow?
By achieving my goals, accepting my challenges and stretching myself beyond what I already know.

By nurturing my determination,
I can see my success will be of my own creation.

My goals are strong and healthy for I
will accept no less; my hard work will
pay off with the growing of my OWN SUCCESS.

V. Rose Kitchen

Creating Your Own Success

are inevitable; are real and in our control. Guess how many fell into the last category? Only 2 percent of all our fears are both real and in our control. And you know what is even better? With action on our part these worries can be solved. So when you find yourself in a panic, figure out which category your fears fall into and then either forget them or take action.

Visualize Success

The following is a very strong aid in reaching goals: Visualize in your mind and in your dreams *who* you want to be and *where* you want to be. Draw this mental picture often until you begin to truly feel it. Once you can create this positive imagery, then subconsciously you will be guided to being what you dream. It should be pointed out that this type of dreaming is the *visualization* of your goals and is very different than daydreaming. Daydreaming is often brought on by boredom and undermines your ability to concentrate if it is not goal oriented.

Chapter 2

More Steps On My Road To Success
A Personal Review

1. What were the key concepts discussed about goals?

2. How do I plan to put this new goal-oriented knowledge into effect?

3. What are the areas I don't understand or need more information on?

4. What is my game plan for getting the additional information I need?

5. What positive changes do I see in myself?

Chapter 2   Goals

Exercise 1 — Goal Sheet 1

**Long-Term Goals —
Life Achievements**

Goal _____

Deadline _____

Steps   1. _____

        2. _____

        3. _____

        4. _____

Goal _____

Deadline _____

Steps   1. _____

        2. _____

        3. _____

        4. _____

Goal _____

Deadline _____

Steps   1. _____

        2. _____

        3. _____

        4. _____

Goal _____

Deadline _____

Steps   1. _____

        2. _____

        3. _____

        4. _____

Chapter 2 Goals

Exercise 2 - Goal Sheet 2

Intermediate Goals — Next 1–5 Years

Goal _____
Deadline _____
Steps 1. _____
2. _____
3. _____
4. _____

Goal _____
Deadline _____
Steps 1. _____
2. _____
3. _____
4. _____

Goal _____
Deadline _____
Steps 1. _____
2. _____
3. _____
4. _____

Goal _____
Deadline _____
Steps 1. _____
2. _____
3. _____
4. _____

Are the above goals on target with my long-term goals?   Yes   No

Creating Your Own Success

Chapter 2 Goals

Exercise 3 - Goal Sheet 3

Short-Term Goals — Specific in the Next Year

Goal _____

Deadline _____

Steps 1. _____

       2. _____

       3. _____

       4. _____

Goal _____

Deadline _____

Steps 1. _____

       2. _____

       3. _____

       4. _____

Goal _____

Deadline _____

Steps 1. _____

       2. _____

       3. _____

       4. _____

Goal _____

Deadline _____

Steps 1. _____

       2. _____

       3. _____

Will my short-term goals help me reach my intermediate and long-term goals?
Yes   No

Chapter 2 Goals

Exercise 4

My Career Goals

Upon graduation I want the following job:

Job title _____

Type of company _____

My responsibilities _____
_____

Skills I will have to learn during school to qualify for this job:

Technical skills: _____
_____
_____
_____

Personal skills: _____
_____
_____
_____

Short-term goals to help me reach these levels of achievement while I'm in school: _____
_____
_____
_____
_____
_____
_____

Creating Your Own Success

Case Study

Yolanda's Dilemma

Yolanda has two small children, no marketable skills, and has to live with her mother and aunt. She wants more for herself and her daughters, but when she mentions getting training, her mother tells her just to be glad to have food on the table and a roof over her head. At that point her aunt always pipes in that it's better not to try to be more than you are.

1. What are the risks if Yolanda listens to her family and doesn't try to improve her life?

2. What are the risks if she does take steps to learn a marketable skill?

3. What would you tell Yolanda to do since there are risks with both options?

4. What ideas are you going to use from your classmates' discussion to motivate yourself?

Chapter 2   Goals

Suggested Resource Material

Books: Additional Resources

Hopkins, Tom. *The Official Guide to Success*. Champion Press Publishing Co., 1983.

Viscott, David. *Risking*. Pocket Books Publishing Co., 1977.

Sheehy, Gail. *Passages*. Bantam Books Publishing Co., 1984.

Ziglar, Zig. *See You at the Top*. Pelican Publishing Co., 1984.

Covey, Stephen R. *The 7 Habits of Highly Effective People*. Simon & Schuster Publishing Co., 1989.

Chapter 3 Listening

"I will learn by listening."

Personal Comment Sheet

Entry Date

Five self-positives:

1.

2.

3.

4.

5.

Getting Focused

How do I think the information I am about to read will help me reach my goals?

It has been said that one pair of ears can empty a thousand tongues.

Do you realize that the majority of our waking hours are spent listening and that more than half the communication people do is listening? This means that what we hear is just as important as what we say or write. Therefore as much effort should be spent on learning to listen as is spent on speaking and writing. Look at all the forms of listening people do — radio, television, presentations, audio learning tapes, stress relaxation tapes, self-help tapes to break bad habits like smoking, just to mention a few. What good are all of these resources if people do not know how to listen actively?

Why Listening Is Important

"I'm sorry, what did you say?" How many times have we all been caught in this very situation. Our eyes have been focused on the speaker's face, our head has been nodding up and down at the appropriate times, and yet we haven't heard a word the other person has said. Sometimes when we're caught, this may just lead to a good laugh among friends; other times it might lead to a fight with a spouse. Or it might even cause us to lose our job. That's right. Often employees lose their jobs because they cannot follow instructions due to poor listening skills. What other problems do poor listening skills cause in relationships, the classroom, or on the job?

Think of how you feel when you find out that someone you are speaking to is not listening. Pretty irritating, right? How do you react when you are talking to someone and they give you their full and undivided attention? It is a pleasant feeling to know that

Figure 3-1

Do these students look like good listeners?

40   **Creating Your Own Success**

the other person is interested and respectful of our thoughts. This skill takes a little practice, but it pays off in a big way. Stronger relationships, better grades, and more job opportunities are just a few of the benefits you'll get by improving your listening skills.

Stumbling Blocks to Listening

Since we know poor listening skills can get us in trouble and good skills give us an edge, why don't we just listen correctly? Unfortunately you may have gotten into some bad habits or not learned to listen correctly in the first place. The good news is you're not alone. Many of us have suffered from one or all of the stumbling blocks below and overcome them. The first step to solving any problem is to recognize it. As you read the following stumbling blocks, put a check mark next to the ones that apply to you.

Daydreaming

One of the biggest obstacles to listening, and probably the hardest to overcome because it comes so naturally, is daydreaming. In Chapter 2 we discussed how to use dreams to visualize your desires and turn your goals into a reality. However, when you are listening you should *not* daydream.

Closed-Mindedness

People often refuse to listen to ideas and opinions that do not match their own. Closing out information will keep the listener from giving a fair appraisal of what is being said.

False Attention

Not really being interested in what someone is saying, but just pretending to listen, is obviously a block to effective listening. Some people are very good at false attention and can usually be spotted because they respond with nods and smiles while you're talking. However, when it becomes their turn to talk, it is obvious they have not been listening.

Hard-to-Understand Subjects

Hard-to-understand subjects often lead to feelings of futility because we tell ourselves that no matter how hard we try, we just can't learn the information. Listen more carefully with an open mind and ask questions whenever possible to check your understanding of the subject matter. It also helps if you make arrangements to discuss the material with a classmate or in a study group.

Memorizing

There are very few individuals with the ability to memorize every spoken word. The more you try to memorize, the less time you actually spend trying to understand the material. Therefore, after the subject has been covered, you may be able to parrot back the information but will not be able to put it into practice effectively.

Rather than attempting to memorize, take good notes and highlight the important sentences and phrases in your books.

Personality Listening

Paying more attention to the speaker's appearance, mannerisms, or grammar than what they have to say is the sixth obstacle to effective listening. As the listener, it is your responsibility to get whatever information you can from every speaker no matter how difficult or boring the job may seem.

Effective Listening Techniques

Even if you placed a check mark next to every one of the stumbling blocks, don't panic. Help is on the way. You've taken an important first step by accepting that you have one or several listening problems. The next step is to actively replace them with the following effective listening techniques. As you find ones that will help you overcome your particular stumbling blocks, put a big star on either side of the heading. Next, write the name of the bad habit that you are going to overcome on that same line. Highlight or underline the sentences or ideas that apply to you. Then put a paper clip or turn back the corner of the pages with the stars on them. At the beginning of every day, refer to these pages until these good habits become second nature.

Figure 3-2

A good listener listens to more than just words.

Listen to More Than Just the Words

Silence is golden. You can learn a lot from people by getting into the habit of watching them while they speak, as they pause to regroup their thoughts, and as they get ready to discuss what you have just said. By not interrupting when someone is speaking, you give the person a chance to give you his/her complete thought on the subject.

Also keep in mind that what is not said may be just as important as what is said. If a person's body language shows anxiety while his or her words sound cheery and happy, you are experiencing a mixed message. This will require you to listen and observe even more closely to interpret the real message. Can you think of a situation where a person's body language contradicted his or her words?

Creating Your Own Success

As the other person speaks, try to identify his or her feelings about the subject being discussed and listen for hidden messages. For example, someone who has never experienced escaping a house fire will discuss the importance of planning an escape route much differently than a person who has had to grope through a blanket of smoke only to find the back door blocked.

Listen Actively

Active listening requires effort on the part of the listener. Just because our ears have picked up noise since we were born, it does not mean we have learned to process these signals correctly. Some of our ears are comparable to an out-of-tune radio. The music is transmitted to the radio correctly but by the time it reaches us it is garbled static. Make a conscious commitment to tune in your ears.

As the other person is speaking, make mental summaries of what he or she is saying. Listen for main ideas and take brief notes if appropriate. Chapter 4 contains additional information on taking notes. Don't assume anything. Give the speaker a chance to explain what he or she means. After the person has completed his or her thoughts, demonstrate that you understand by paraphrasing what was said.

Ask Questions

After the person has stopped speaking, you may ask questions or add your thoughts. Use good questioning techniques to improve your understanding of what the person was trying to say. Remember, communication is not a combat sport with winners and losers. Your goal in questioning is not to show how smart you are or to put the speaker on the defensive. Instead, phrase your question so that with his or her answer you will more fully understand the information the speaker has shared.

Listen with More Than Just Your Ears

Good eye contact while you are listening helps you concentrate and keeps your mind from wandering off to Tahiti or some other dream island. Remember that listening is done with your eyes as well as your ears. Communication is 10% words, 35% voice tone, and 55% nonverbal. By watching the speaker you are listening to body language, which will be covered in more detail in Chapter 9. Nevertheless, don't stare while you are listening or let yourself become hypnotized by the speaker's voice or mannerisms.

As you listen, also involve your heart. Try to understand why the person speaking may feel the way he or she does. Rather than jumping to conclusions, allowing emotions like anger, fear, frustration, or resentment to interfere; or instead of becoming defensive, relax and ask yourself what this person's words mean to him or her. Stop before you speak and try to picture why this person might feel the way he or she does, and then find a common ground or understanding before you begin to express your ideas. Don't allow past experiences to prevent you from listening effectively. Has anyone ever refused to listen to your words because of their preconceived notions? Automatically lumping people together in groups before you hear what they have to say hampers your ability to listen effectively by telling your brain in advance what to expect from "this type of person."

Listen Smart

Choose the right people to listen to when it comes to advice, consultation, and statements about you and your abilities. Learn to filter out negative messages that hurt your chances for success. Remember that just because you hear a message doesn't mean you have to accept it as truth. Get in the habit of thinking through what you hear and deciding for yourself if it makes sense.

Exercise Your Listening

In understanding exactly what listening is, you must realize that it is an activity — a skill that requires active participation. Here are two simple exercises that will help you practice your active listening skills.

Listen to the Words and the Emotions

While watching and listening to a movie or the news, repeat to yourself exactly what the newscaster or character just said. After a while, practice not just repeating the line but also feeling the emotion attached to it.

Listen to the Sounds

While sitting or reclining, close your eyes and concentrate on listening for every sound. Use the following blank space to write down sounds that you hear — a train far off, an owl, a bird singing, the subway, a drippy faucet, or a barking dog. After a while you will find yourself hearing sounds that in the past you were not aware of.

Creating Your Own Success

Chapter 3

More Steps On My Road To Success
A Personal Review

1. What were the key concepts discussed about listening effectively?

2. How do I plan to put my new listening knowledge into effect?

3. What are the areas I don't understand or need more information on?

4. What is my game plan for getting the additional information I need?

5. What positive changes do I see in myself?

Chapter 3 Listening

Exercises 1–2

Being aware of an obstacle is the first step in overcoming it. If any of the following obstacles is a barrier to your listening growth, put a check mark by it. Under each obstacle you have checked, write a note to yourself on how you plan to tackle this barrier. After you write it, reread it; then repeat it to yourself. Decide to make a conscious effort to eliminate this barrier to your listening growth.

1. _____ Daydreaming

_____
_____
_____
_____

2. _____ Closed-Mindedness

_____
_____
_____
_____

3. _____ False Attention

_____
_____
_____
_____

Creating Your Own Success

4. _____ Hard-to-Understand Subjects

5. _____ Memorizing

6. _____ Personality Listening

Chapter 3 Listening

Exercise 3

As a listening exercise your instructor is going to read you a short story and then have you answer a list of questions. Please enter your answers below.

1. _____

2. _____

3. _____

4. _____

5. _____

6. _____

7. _____

8. _____

9. _____

10. _____

Chapter 3   Listening

Exercise 4

Below is a partial outline of your listening chapter. Compare it to the chapter headings and the information underneath each heading. You can see that the outline highlights only the main ideas. As you study this example of how an outline is written, fill in the blank spaces. This will help you lock the information that you have just studied deeper into your brain.

Outline

Listening

I. Why Listening Is _____

    A. Time Spent Listening

        1. Majority of our _____ hours

        2. More than half of the _____ people do is listening

        3. I should spend just as much time learning to listen as

           I spend on _____ and _____

    B. A Few Forms of Listening People Do

        1. _____

        2. _____

        3. _____

        4. _____

II. Stumbling Blocks to Listening

    A. Daydreaming
        1. One of the biggest obstacles and probably the

           _____ to overcome

        2. When listening, do _____ daydream

B. _____ Mindedness

    1. A difference of _____

    2. Can't give a fair _____ of what's being said

C. False Attention

    1. Lack of _____ in what is being said

    2. _____ to listen

D. Hard-to-Understand Subjects

    1. Listen more _____ with an open mind

    2. Ask _____ whenever possible

E. Memorizing

    1. Very difficult to _____ every spoken word

    2. Take good _____ and highlight _____ sentences

F. Personality Listening

    1. Paying too much attention to the speaker's

        a. appearance

        b. _____

        c. _____

    2. My _____ to get whatever information I can

III. Effective Listening Techniques

  A. Listen to More Than Just the Words

    1. Allow _____ to give _____ thoughts on subject

    2. Speaker's _____ language says a lot

    3. Identify speaker's feelings; listen for hidden _____

B. Listen Actively

    1. Tune in your _____ to speaker

    2. Make mental _____ of what is said

    3. Give the speaker a chance to _____ meaning

C. Ask Questions

    1. Use good _____ techniques

    2. Remember, communication is not a _____ sport

    3. Try not to put the speaker on the _____

D. Listen with More Than Just Your Ears

    1. Have good _____ contact, but do not _____

    2. Don't jump to _____

    3. Don't allow past _____ to interfere

E. Listen Smart

    1. Choose the _____ people to listen to

    2. Learn to _____ out negative messages

    3. Get in the habit of _____ through what you hear

Case Study

Ernesto Is Always in a Hurry

While people talk to Ernesto, his mind races to come up with a good answer. His boss, Mrs. Chou, has just finished asking him for a detailed list of computer documents that she wants printed out before the owner arrives. Ernesto nods his head with each request as he thinks of the best way to format the documents. When he returns to his office, he writes down the document names she wants done. But in trying to remember the conversation, he comes up with only five, when he is certain that she asked for eight. Sitting down at his computer, he mumbles angrily that she should be more clear in her directions.

1. What does Ernesto need to do to improve his listening skills?

2. What should Ernesto do now?

3. What could Mrs. Chou have done to avoid this problem?

Suggested Resource Material

Books: Additional Resources

Augsburger, David. *Caring Enough to Hear and Be Heard.* Herald Press Publishing Co., 1982.

Murphy, Kevin J. *Effective Listening: Hearing What People Say and Putting It to Work for You.* Bantam Publishing Co., 1989.

Dominick, Barbara. *The Art Of Listening.* C C Thomas Publishing Co., 1974.

Burley-Allen, Madelyn. *Listening: The Forgotten Skill.* Wiley Publishing Co., 1987.

Chapter 4
Reading and Taking Notes

"I enjoy filling my mind with new information by reading and listening."

Personal Comment Sheet

Entry Date

Five self-positives:

1.

2.

3.

4.

5.

Getting Focused

How do I think the information I am about to read will help me reach my goals?

Would you like to understand more of what you read? This chapter will show you how to pick out important information and will explain the types of reading. In addition, you will learn how to lock in the information you read by reviewing.

Would you like to learn to cut down on your study time and still increase your grades? Effective note taking can help you do just that. The second part of this chapter is going to cover how to take notes so that when you study you are using your time effectively. In addition, you will practice your note-taking skills at the end of this chapter.

Reading

This skill consumes more time than any other activity related to studying. Reading effectively requires concentration and using as many of your five senses as possible.

Reading should never be approached as a passive activity. Effective reading requires total mental and physical involvement.

Basic Parts of a Book

When we get ready to take a trip, most of us begin by looking at a map. Reading a book is also like taking a trip. By reading the words on a page we can go back in time, learn about other cultures, gain new skills, or travel to places that don't even exist. Just as with any trip, to get the most out of our journey we should start by looking at a map. In the case of a textbook our map is made up of the various parts of a book.

Figure 4-1

Reading effectively requires concentration.

Preface or Introduction

This is usually found in the front of the book and gives the author a chance to speak directly to the reader. In the preface, the author may explain his or her purpose for writing the book, tell you how best to approach the information contained in the book, or just share some personal experiences. By reading this section you will be picking up clues about what to expect.

Table of Contents

This list shows the chapter titles and gives you the page number for the beginning of each chapter. By skimming this section you will learn what major subjects will be covered. As you study the table of contents, ask yourself why the author chose to present the information in that particular order. Since with most textbooks each chapter builds to help complete your knowledge on a subject, as you finish reading the chapter titles in this book try to summarize how the information presented will help you reach your goals.

Chapters or Lessons

This is the meat of the book. In your chapters or lessons you will find the information that will help increase your skills and knowledge.

Appendix

The appendix contains supplemental information at the end of the book. It may contain the glossary, the bibliography, contacts for additional information, or a detailed list of books or articles that are referred to in the text of the book. By looking at this section you will learn where you can go to find additional information.

Glossary

This section may be found at the back of the book, at the end of each chapter, or may be part of the appendix. The glossary lists and defines the key words used in the book. By studying the glossary, you will improve your understanding of the subject matter. When you come upon a new key word, turn to the glossary and look it up, even if you think you know the meaning. You may find that the author is using it in a different way.

Bibliography

The bibliography, at the end of the book, lists books or articles that will give you more information on the subject you are studying. How can you use this material? We've all read new information and found it impossible to understand. By turning to one of these additional resources, you may find just the explanation you need to clear things up. In addition, by studying a variety of books and articles you strengthen your understanding of the subject matter.

Index

This is usually the last part of the book and provides the reader with an alphabetical list of all the main topics covered in the book. By looking over these pages quickly, you will get a good overview of what the book covers. Also, when you are in a hurry to find specific information, this is the best place to start.

Types of Reading

You love college football. You can't wait for the season to begin so you can devour the sports section of your local newspaper. As you turn to that part of the paper, you scan the article about a local business that just received an award. Turning to the stock pages, you skim down a list of stock prices. Disgusted, you turn to the sports section, sit back with a cup of coffee, and take your phone off the hook.

Our college football fanatic has just used all three types of reading. Can you spot them?

Skimming

This is used most frequently when you just want to get the main ideas or when you first open a book to a new chapter. By reading the introduction, the headings, and the final paragraph, you can usually pick out the general ideas. As you skim, write down a list of questions you want to find the answers to during your in-depth reading of the material. This gets your mind ready to learn more about the subject.

Scanning

When you scan you are looking for specific information. In our example the article about the local business was scanned. What types of information would a businessperson have scanned for in this article? Probably they would have wanted to know the type of award, type of business, if they were competitors, or if there was any way this award could open the door for the two of them to do business together. When will you most likely scan information? This form of reading will be used when reviewing your chapters and notes.

In-depth Reading

Use this form of reading when you want to understand and recall all of the major facts contained in the material. After you have skimmed a new chapter, you will then be ready for an in-depth read. Make sure you have the questions you developed during the skimming stage handy so that you can look for their answers as you read.

Preparing Mentally for Effective Reading

Before you begin to read you should think about the purpose of the reading assignment. Reading for information and facts requires more concentration and effort than reading a book for pleasure. You should relate the reading assignment to what you want to achieve; for example, new information that will help you reach career goals. Also, relate this new information to what you already know. For example, if you are reading your first chapter in Accounting II, tie this new information directly into what you learned in Accounting I.

Let's Read

By reading the table of contents you're sure you've got a firm grasp on the big picture. You've decided to follow our advice and skim the chapter first and then do an in-depth read. So what's the hold-up? You guessed it. There are still a few more things you can do to improve your reading ability.

Get Physically Ready to Read

Physically, you should be in a comfortable position for reading, but not so comfortable you fall asleep. For example, the bed is not a good place for reading because subconsciously your mind tells you this is the place to sleep.

Select an area with good light to reduce eye strain and plan scheduled breaks.

Sitting and reading for long periods of time can be tedious, so change positions. Stand up and move around. Surprising as it may seem, you can read on your feet.

Don't forget to turn wasted time into reading time. For example, you can read while waiting for the bus, on the subway, and while doing laundry. This gives you a good chance to accomplish two things simultaneously.

Preview the Chapter

Skim through the reading material by examining each page of the chapter. You should look at paragraph headings, graphs, charts, and any visuals that help to explain the information. Remember to ask yourself as you skim how this information will help you reach your goals. Pay close attention to chapter summaries. A summary will give you information on the main points of the chapter. Also, notice if there are questions at the end of the chapter. These questions will provide a guideline as to the information you should concentrate on while reading.

In the event there are no summaries, create an outline as you are reading using section titles. By skimming this chapter, you already know we will talk about this in more detail later and that you will practice your outlining skill in Exercise 1.

Decide What Is Important

If it is possible to write in the text, then highlight, underline, and jot notes in the margins. However, do not get carried away and lose the point of highlighting and underlining. You should only highlight or underline key words or ideas. Highlighting entire sentences prevents you from easily picking out the key ideas. To insure that you don't get carried away with that neon pen, try reading a paragraph first and then going back and highlighting. By doing this, you know what the key ideas are before you mark in your book. For example, if these sentences were part of your text, you would only need to highlight the underlined words to capture the main ideas.

<u>Oprah Winfrey</u> did **<u>not grow up</u>** with **<u>wealth</u>** or **<u>powerful connections</u>** in the TV industry. But this **<u>did not stop her.</u>** She was **<u>determined to succeed</u>** and did so by **<u>working hard</u>** and **<u>smart,</u>** and never losing sight of her **<u>goals.</u>**

Chapter 4   **Reading and Taking Notes**

What should you write in the margin of your books? Anything that helps you understand and retain the information. Mark your questions, jot key ideas from your notes, or write the definitions of glossary terms.

Review What You Read

You should plan to read the information more than once. By reading it the first time to yourself, then going back a second time and reading it aloud, you will retain more information. You will find it easier to lock in information when you involve as many of your five senses as possible.

How often should you review and when? Reviewing the material within twenty-four hours of when you first read it gives your brain the best chance to absorb it. Then make it a habit to review the material on both a weekly and monthly basis. If you have read the chapter the night before, reviewing it right before class will help you understand the instructor's lecture. Again at the end of class, review any new material that was covered. There is no substitute for reviewing.

Another way to review is to read the assignment aloud, taping the key ideas and sample questions. This type of review can benefit you in several ways. Listening to the information read in your own voice can help you to absorb it more completely. When you do this you are seeing the information, saying it, and hearing it. Also, this allows you to turn wasted time into productive time. You can listen to your tape as you are traveling back and forth to school, getting ready in the morning, or fixing meals. The tape may not be quite as entertaining as the latest hit song, but knowing the words on your tape will certainly help you more in the long run.

Study Further

All of us have stumbled on a new word when we are reading. When this happens, try to figure out what the word means by using the rest of the sentence as a guide. Then grab your dictionary and see if you were right. Developing a good vocabulary will aid in understanding what you are reading.

Use bibliographies for alternate reading material. Sometimes using another source on the same subject will make the information clearer.

Ask Help from Others

When you are really confused, ask your instructor for help.

Study groups can be very beneficial. Before you join a study group, sit in a couple of times and see if everyone is participating equally. It is not in your best interest to get involved if only a few are doing all of the work or talking. Once you do join, come prepared to ask questions and relate interpretations. Brainstorming a reading assignment can be fun. Especially if you throw in a couple of pizzas.

Notes

Tossing and turning, Sheila pictures the instructor laughing as she hands out the final exam. Frightened, she jumps out of bed. Frantically digging out a pencil and some paper, she tries to remember what the instructor talked about in class. But it's no use. Pulling out little pieces of hair, she sobs aloud that next time she'll take notes. Her screams of anguish wake up the entire neighborhood.

Some of you may have already felt a little like Sheila when you were studying for a test. This next section will show you how to avoid those sleepless nights spent trying to remember what was said in class.

Reasons for Taking Notes

Notes are a reinforcement for memory recall. Most people are like Sheila and cannot remember everything they read or hear. What are some of the other reasons for taking notes?

Positive Attitude

When you come to class ready to take notes, you are mentally preparing yourself to learn.

Effective Use of Time

Taking notes enables you to save time that would be used looking up information. Taking notes and learning more in class means spending less time on the subject out of class.

If the school does not allow you to highlight or underline a book, then you can add key points from the chapter to your notes.

Improved Listening

Notes are a reinforcement for listening and paying attention. It is impossible to catch the important points of a lecture if you are not concentrating and listening.

Figure 4-2

Notes reinforce our memory.

Chapter 4 — Reading and Taking Notes

Taking notes means you are writing and listening, thus using two of your five senses. Note taking is active involvement, which learning requires.

Easy Review

To help you prepare for tests, use your notes when you review. There are some tests (for instance, open-book tests) in which you can use your notes during the test.

When should you review your notes? Review them as soon after class as possible. At this time correct any misspelled words, add missing words or key ideas, and interpret any sloppy handwriting. If your handwriting is hard to read, this last part is time well spent. Otherwise, when you look at your notes later you may wonder how a chicken managed to scratch all over your papers. If you find that you are spending very much time rewriting, try printing during the lectures. Then make it a habit to review your notes, at a minimum, at the end of the week and at the end of the month.

Better Understanding

Your notes allow you to separate the major points from minor ones. They also help you compare what you heard in class with the information in your textbook.

Taking Notes

Now that you know why taking notes is important, let's look at some keys to effective note taking.

In the Classroom

In the classroom setting you will be taking notes from your instructor's lecture and from the group discussions.

Key Words

It is not necessary or desirable for you to write every word spoken. Instead, you should only record the main points. For example, if your instructor says, "We have probably all heard the old saying 'You are what you eat,' but it is even more true that we are what we think. Our mind controls our feelings, our attitudes, and chances for success," your notes would look like this:

> You are what you think.
> Mind controls — feelings — attitudes — chance for success.

As you can see, these few words sum up the key ideas.

Searching for Clues

By reading the material before class and completing your assignments, you will have already picked up some clues as to the

Creating Your Own Success

important information. If, as the instructor lectures, you notice that he/she is keying in on all chapter headings, this signals an area you can concentrate on. If you had not read the chapter in advance, you would have missed this significant clue.

Throughout your instructors' lectures, they will be giving you clues about what they consider to be the most important information. As they are talking, be aware of facial expressions, body language, and tone of voice. Are they excited, are they leaning over the podium, have they gotten up and started writing on the board, have they repeated an idea or concept more than once? All of these can signal that the information is important.

Listen closely for words and phrases like "It is important to remember," "The major consideration is," "especially," "in addition to," and of course the obvious, "This will be on the test." When you hear any of these signals it's a good time to take notes.

From the Textbook

By supplementing your lecture notes with notes from your textbook you are taking maximum advantage of your learning opportunity. When taking notes from the textbook, write down only key ideas and words. Just as with lecture notes, it is not necessary to write down every word.

Summarize

By writing out the key headings and putting in your own words what you know about those topics, you will help spot weak areas. For example, if one of your main headings is Short-Term Goals, you would write down everything you remembered about this subject. Then you would flip back to the material and add any key information that you missed. This type of review helps you build on what you already know and strengthens your understanding of the material. Also, summarizing information in your own words sometimes helps you remember it more easily.

Developing an Outline

When you are writing notes from your textbooks, you are looking for key ideas. The easiest way to keep these key ideas in order is to develop an outline. In your Chapter 3 exercises you completed an outline of that chapter. As this exercise showed, you use the headings in the chapter as a guide. These headings are listed as Roman numerals. After you write your heading, list a brief phrase or word underneath that explains the key idea in more detail. This information takes the form of an alphabetic listing underneath the Roman numeral. Flip now to Exercise 1 on page 67 for an example.

Developing Your Own Style

Developing your own note-taking style will save you time. If you know shorthand or speed writing then notes should be a breeze.

But what about those of us who don't? The following ideas will help you take notes like a pro.

Keep It Simple

By using abbreviations, acronyms, and symbols, you will save time. For example, instead of writing out "as soon as possible" people use ASAP. Or they will substitute for the word "with" by just writing w/. What other words can you think of that can be abbreviated or turned into acronyms?

Another time saver is to eliminate unnecessary words like "a," "and," "the," and also punctuation. And remember to write down only key words and ideas, not entire sentences.

Lots of Blank Space

When taking notes, many of us try to cram as much on a page as possible. But then when we go back to review or make corrections we have nowhere to write this information. Before you begin to take notes, draw a line one and a half to two inches from the left margin. During your initial note taking, leave this area blank. Then when you go back to review, you have this section to write

Figure 4-3

Notes will help you study more efficiently.

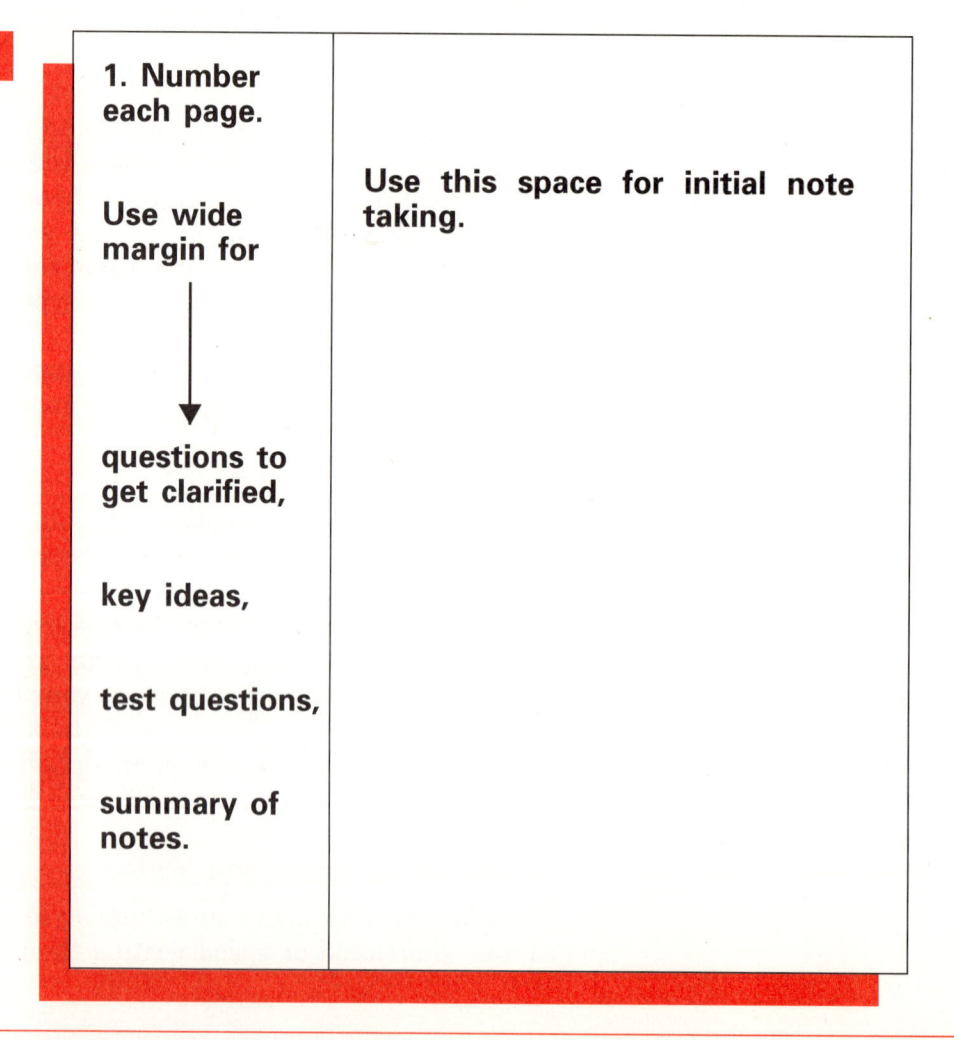

1. Number each page. **Use wide margin for** ↓ **questions to get clarified,** **key ideas,** **test questions,** **summary of notes.**	**Use this space for initial note taking.**

in questions to get clarified, key ideas, and sample test questions. In other words, you now have a place to take notes on your notes. Right now some of you are groaning and grumbling that once was enough. But remember, the idea of notes is to study more efficiently and get better grades. How does taking notes a second time help you? By summarizing your notes in the wide left margin, when reviewing, you can cover up your more detailed notes on the right. Then by asking yourself questions you can quickly and efficiently check your understanding of the material.

But what if you turn to one of your additional resource books and want to add even more information? This is the main reason for only writing on the front of your paper. Again, this insures that you have lots of blank paper if you need it without having your notes scattered throughout six different notebooks. Seriously, we have seen students try to study this way and it wasn't a pretty sight.

Keep Them Organized

Have you ever had a three-ring binder come undone? It can take hours to get your papers back in order. But you won't have that problem if you just take a little time before class to start your notes off right. At the top of the first page, write out the class name, the date, your name, and the number one. Then, for every page after this one, continue to number the pages in sequence.

Practice, Practice, Practice

As with any new skill the only way to get really good is to practice. You are already getting several chances to apply your new skill in your classes. But there is another way that you can sharpen your personal note-taking style. Practice taking notes of the dialogue on TV programs as you watch them. The news is particularly good for this since it consists of almost all talk. Practicing while watching TV or listening to the radio will not only strengthen your note-taking skills, it will also help you work on your listening skills.

Chapter 4

More Steps On My Road To Success
A Personal Review

1. a. What were the key concepts discussed about reading?

   b. What were the key concepts discussed about taking notes?

2. How do I plan to use my new reading and note-taking skills to help me reach my goals?

3. What are the areas I don't understand or need more information on?

4. What is my game plan for getting the additional information I need?

5. What positive changes do I see in myself?

Chapter 4   Reading and Taking Notes

Exercise 1

In the Listening chapter, we gave you a partial outline which you used to learn more about how to develop a study outline. In this exercise we are going to take you a step further by having you complete the entire chapter outline. Don't panic; we have given you the basic form that will help guide you as to how many key ideas to look for under each heading. Remember, outlining is a great way to lock information deeper into your brain.

OUTLINE

I. Reading

    A. Basic Parts of a Book

        1. _____

        2. _____

        3. _____

        4. _____

        5. _____

        6. _____

        7. _____

    B. Types of Reading

        1. _____

        2. _____

        3. _____

    C. Preparing Mentally for Effective Reading

        1. _____

        2. _____

        3. _____

        4. _____

5. _____
6. _____
7. _____

II. Notes

   A. Reasons for Taking Notes

      1. _____
      2. _____
      3. _____
      4. _____
      5. _____

   B. Taking Notes

      1. In the Classroom

         a. _____
         b. _____

      2. From Textbook

         a. _____
         b. _____

   C. Developing Your Own Style

      1. _____
      2. _____
      3. _____
      4. _____

Chapter 4 Reading and Taking Notes

Exercise 2

For practice, highlight the key concepts in this paragraph.

General Colin Powell did not follow the traditional stop at West Point on his trip to Chairman of the Joint Chiefs of Staff position. Instead, born to Jamaican immigrants who lived in Harlem, he completed the ROTC program at City College of New York. His bravery in Vietnam, and his understanding of the politics of Washington, D.C. helped him rise quickly to prominence. Instead of using his background as an excuse as to why he couldn't become a general, he took responsibility for his own life and made his dreams reality.

Chapter 4 Reading and Taking Notes

Exercise 3

For practice take notes from the following paragraph.

Steve Guttenburg, an actor known for his roles in the movies *Three Men and a Baby* and *Three Men and a Little Lady*, could sit back and enjoy the easy life in California. Instead, on Sunday mornings he gives his time, effort, and caring to people less fortunate than himself. Buying bread, meat, cheese, fruit, and cookies, he makes up fifty lunches and then hands them out to the homeless.

Case Study

It Just Doesn't Add Up

Brian has just failed his first math test. He needs the class to graduate and is upset because he did so poorly. In an effort to help him, his instructor, Mr. Goldberg, sat down with him and discussed his reading and note-taking habits. Here is a copy of Mr. Goldberg's notes and his personal observations:

6/12 — Brian having trouble in Math101. Reads the chapters while watching TV. Does only the assigned problems and these usually completed in the student lounge right before class. Sits back of classroom — doesn't ask questions — homework sloppy. Says he's never been good at math — neither is his father. Notes from class are taken on scraps of paper and stuffed in front of book.

If you were Mr. Goldberg, what steps would you suggest Brian take in the areas of study skills and self-awareness to increase his chances for success?

Suggested Resource Material

Books: Additional Resources

Root, Jane H. *Read On!* Basic Reading for Adults and Teens. Literacy Volunteers of America, Inc. Syracuse, NY, 1987.

Case, Angelica W. *Reading Power.* Arco Publishing Co., 1984.

Fossard, Esta de. *Reading in Focus: Learning to Get the Message.* South-Western Publishing Co., 1989.

Fossard, Esta de. *Food for Thought: Reading and Thinking Critically.* South-Western Publishing Co., 1992.

Sire, James W. *How to Read Slowly: Reading for Comprehension.* Shaw Publishing Co., 1989.

Agardy, Franklin J. *How to Read Faster & Better.* Arco Publishing Co., 1983.

Chapter 5 Attitudes

"I will focus on the best in the people and situations that life hands me."

Personal Comment Sheet

Entry Date

Five self-positives:

1.

2.

3.

4.

5.

Getting Focused

How do I think the information I am about to read will help me reach my goals?

Attitudes

Only part of your growth is based on ability; the other part is based on attitude. Your attitudes have been formed over many years by a variety of experiences and messages. But though outside influences have helped form your attitudes, they are entirely under your control. Each of us has the power, if we will use it, to change our attitudes so they help us reach our goals.

Since attitude development is an ongoing process, you must accept that there are no quick fixes. None of us is ever a finished product. Realizing that attitudes are not acquired overnight nor are they inherited means that as much time must be spent on developing positive attitudes as was spent on developing negative ones.

Understanding Attitudes

Most attitudes fit into one of two categories. They either add to our enjoyment of life and help us reach our goals or they have a negative effect on our life and hurt our chances for success.

Figure 5-1

Who has the positive attitude?

Attitudes That Hurt Us

Sam has very poor attendance and, because of this, his grades are low. When his classmates or instructors try to help he gets angry and tells them to leave him alone. The few times he does talk in class it is to make a negative comment or put another student down.

It's easy to see that Sam's negative attitudes are hurting his chances for success. Like many people with negative attitudes, he doesn't realize his attitudes are self-defeating. He has responded to life this way so long that he isn't aware he is hurting himself.

Creating Your Own Success

But if we can see it, why can't he? It's always hard to look at ourselves honestly, but it is the first step toward taking responsibility for our attitudes. Sometimes it helps to start this process by looking at others. By studying other people, it is usually easier for you to see what attitudes you have in common and whether they are positive or negative.

As children we experience many emotions — happiness, sadness, anger, rejection — and begin to form a mental image of ourselves based on our dealings with our families, teachers, and others who helped mold our formative years. If we receive more of one kind of experience than we do another, our attitudes may begin to develop in that direction. If we experience more stressful and unhappy emotions during this conditioning and are never taught to deal with these emotions then we as adults see ourselves as victims. Being a victim isn't any fun. Replacing your negative attitudes with those that empower you will go a long way to making you feel more like a victor than a victim.

Take time now to look at the messages adults sent you as a child and make a conscious decision to accept or reject this information. Do not continue living your life based on misinformation.

Attitudes That Help Us

Experience shows that people gravitate toward people with a good attitude. You see it everywhere — at a bus stop, the bank, or the supermarket. These people are always smiling and have a good word for everyone they meet. You won't find them complaining or criticizing and putting others on the defensive. If they have a problem, they look at how it can be solved — not why it can't be.

These types of attitudes make people want to be around you and greatly increase your chances for success. What examples can you think of where someone's positive attitude made you feel better?

Success Doesn't Always Mean Winning

It is easy to make the mistake of confusing winning and success. But they are two different things. Success does not always mean you are a winner. If you stole another student's report, you might pass the class. But you would not be a winner because you would have cheated yourself out of the knowledge that doing the report would have given you.

"Winners" and "Losers" are just labels carelessly used to describe the person who comes in first and the person who comes in last. The person who comes in last is not a loser, because he or she tried and didn't quit. In addition, if that person learned from the experience, he or she just boosted their chances for success in the future. This makes that person a double winner. The only real losers in life are those people who give up on themselves.

Figure 5-2

> **Attitudes**
>
> A good attitude for everyone to see, is the image I want for me.
> To roll with the punches, and start each day with a smile.
> Not just thinking about myself, but sensitive to others who may need my help.
> I won't be afraid to take a chance my attitude will show:
> I must take risks if my success is to grow.
> If I fail along the way, then I will just try harder another day.
>
> by
> V. Rose Kitchen

Remember, everything you hope to achieve must start with the proper attitude.

Turning Your Attitudes Around

You've accepted that your attitudes are in your control. After looking at yourself and other people, you've picked out some attitudes that you need to change. But now what do you do?

Identify Why You Have a Negative Attitude

Figuring out where your negative attitude may have come from is a good first step. If your great-Aunt Minnie told you repeatedly when you were little that all men are bums, it wouldn't be surprising for you to have trouble in your relationships with men. You would simply be acting on great-Aunt Minnie's message.

But what if you have a negative attitude toward a class? Surely, your great-Aunt Minnie didn't make you hate English, too. Most of the time when you have a negative attitude toward a class it's because you don't like it, not because you can't do it. How do you change this attitude? Look at how the class is going to help you achieve what you want, and then do the best you can. This is a positive attitude adjustment. Successful people make these kinds of adjustments all the time. They don't give up on things just because they don't like them or because they are hard or unpleasant. Instead, they try to get everything they can from the experience, in the certainty they will use the information at some point in time. They've learned that every lesson life hands us has value, and that part of growing is accepting the good with the bad.

Don't Fall Victim to Negative Conditioning

You realize that great-Aunt Minnie was wrong. All men are not bums. But although you know this isn't true, sometimes you find it hard not to act as if it is. This is what happens when we fall victim to negative conditioning.

There's a story about grasshoppers, which is an excellent example of this conditioning. The grasshoppers were placed in a glass jar and a lid was placed on top of the jar. The grasshoppers jumped up, hitting the lid over and over trying to get out of the jar, and each time their bodies hit the lid they fell back to the bottom of the jar. Finally, they stopped jumping so high to avoid hitting the lid. The lid was removed from the jar, offering the grasshoppers freedom, but they did not attempt to jump any higher than they had with the lid on. They were so conditioned, they believed nothing could be any different.

How do you make sure you're not a grasshopper? Going to school gives you a great chance to learn new skills, have new experiences, and meet new people. Take advantage of these opportunities even if at first you feel uncomfortable. Drown out any of your internal negative attitudes that try to hurt your chances of reaching your goal. Until you have replaced these negative attitudes with positive ones — and this will take some time — just block those negative attitudes by reminding yourself that you refuse to be a grasshopper. And keep on your aggressive program of positive replacement.

Strive Toward Positive Attitudes

Each person must have the desire to become a successful person with positive attitudes that are open and innovative. No one can do this for you. But you can learn from the example of others. What attitudes do positive people share? They are not afraid of failure; if it doesn't work the first time, they try again. They have an awareness of reality and know that often it doesn't meet their expectations, but they continue to move forward. They have learned that negative attitudes are like brick walls that are constructed over a long time. They also know they cannot wait for someone else to tear down the wall before changes can occur. In addition to taking responsibility for their attitudes, they have studied human nature so they can use this knowledge to help them reach their goals.

Guidelines in Human Relations

We all have different personalities, past experiences, and outlooks on life. But although each of us is unique, we share similar ways of behaving. These behaviors are commonly called human nature.

Understanding and using the following guidelines will greatly improve your chances for success.

Attitudes Are Visible

People judge your attitude by more than just your words. The first thing we notice is a person's outward personality. For example, you have just been introduced to Mary. She is smiling and looks excited to meet you. You will probably view Mary as having a positive attitude. What if Mary had frowned, shrugged her shoulders when you were introduced, and refused to shake your hand? You might give her a second chance, but your initial impression probably would not be positive. Yet both Mary's did not say one word in our example. You decided which was positive and which was negative just by judging visible signs.

What is an easy way to make your positive attitude visible? Smile. That's right. A simple genuine smile goes a long way to showing a good attitude. Give a smile away today and then report in class what happened.

Treat People Fairly

When dealing with people, treat others as you would like to be treated. Remember the Golden Rule? Though this guideline is easy to remember, it is sometimes hard to live. How do you put this guideline into practice? Before you act, take a second to put yourself in the other person's place. Then ask yourself how you would want to be treated. Don't be surprised if sometimes your kindness is not returned, for others may not follow these guidelines. And also don't let their negative response cause you to give up. Over time other people will notice your positive attitude and it will help you succeed.

Use a Little Honey

Insects are drawn to something sweet. Humans are drawn to kindness. Try an experiment: Select someone who has been rude or unreceptive to you, and for one week respond to that person with kindness and consideration no matter what. In class tell the outcome of your experiment. No names need to be used; simply report the reactions of the other person.

When in a confrontation situation, this guideline still applies. It is very difficult to argue with someone who will not argue back, and very difficult to be rude to someone that will not give you that power over them. People who refuse to argue know that there are no winners, only hurt feelings.

Help Other People Win

People respond to a "you can" attitude. If you help people to believe in themselves, then you help to give them something good to live up to.

It's a fact that the people we like to do business with are the people who try to see things from our point of view. They listen to us and sympathize with us and offer constructive advice to help us.

Keep Some Things to Yourself

In certain situations it is best to keep your thoughts to yourself. This is particularly true in the areas of criticism and complaining.

Criticism is a two-edged sword; if you are going to give it, then be prepared to receive it. It's not so much what you say but how you say it; in other words, use diplomacy. Being critical of others continually is really putting our own flaws on display. Putting it bluntly: Bad-mouthing someone doesn't make them look bad, it makes *you* look bad. Over the next few days watch someone who is always critical of others and see how people respond to them.

What should you do if you have to point out a problem area? Always keep it on a professional level and point out at least one positive thing about the person or their performance. Try saying "Well, that's one way of looking at it. Now let's try another way" or "You did a super job, but that's not quite what I'm looking for."

Have you noticed how many people love to complain? These people have no self-control. They are the ones who look for problems instead of answers, or make "mountains out of mole hills" just to look important. Complaining about a situation won't solve the situation, but looking at our choices will. Accept it or change it.

Remember, creating new attitudes can be frustrating, but the results are worth it.

Freckles or Warts

Another area of attitudes deals with how we turn freckles into warts. These are all the small problems we turn into catastrophes, treating each problem as a life or death episode. Looking at these problems rationally instead of emotionally, we can easily see them for what they are. If you spill the sugar bowl you know you must clean it up. Of course there is the loss of the sugar, but by not letting yourself get angry and stressed over what has happened you are dealing with it rationally. You are treating it simply as an inconvenience, rather than allowing it to ruin your day.

I remember one orientation for new students. I was one of the speakers at this orientation. The day before I was suppose to speak, an insect had stung me, using my eye as its target. I had an allergic reaction, which caused my eye to swell shut. To make matters worse, the side of my face was also swollen. My first reaction was of horror at the thought of standing up there in front of a large group of new students looking like Popeye's twin sister. I wanted to get out of the speech and hide somewhere. But after looking at it rationally I realized I wasn't in any pain, and I just looked funny — which was an inconvenience, not the end of the world. I spoke at that orientation, explaining that I had not been in a fight and I was not kin to Popeye. Actually it turned out to be a very successful speech, and I heard hundreds of stories about insect bites from the new students. Can you think of a time when you have reacted this way?

Make a point to stop overreacting to inconveniences and it will help your attitude tremendously. Note these inconveniences in your life and ask yourself if this is a freckle or a wart before reacting.

Figure 5-3

Stop overreacting to inconveniences and it will help your attitude.

Your Mind and Your Attitude

For many of us, our attitudes are affected by how we feel. We get up in the morning and can't find anything to wear or our alarm clock doesn't work so we oversleep and are late. We tell ourselves "Boy, this is going to be another lousy day." We are letting one or two events color the entire rest of our day. Even worse, some of us have let just one or two events color our entire life; for example, we let one unhappy marriage convince us that all members of the opposite sex are jerks.

We have probably all heard the old saying "You are what you eat," but it is even more true that WE ARE WHAT WE THINK. Our minds control our feelings, attitudes, and chances for success. If we choose to be negative, our mind will search for all of the negative information it can find to help us reach our goal of feeling

Creating Your Own Success

negative. On the other hand, if we choose to be a positive person, our mind can be retrained to find all the positive information that we need to reach our goal.

The key concept to remember is that the mind can't tell the difference between a real experience and an experience that is imagined repeatedly in as much detail as possible. This is why it is very important to look at your goal posters every day and vividly imagine your life once you reach your goals.

Positive Self-Talk

Not only do you need to be aware of how powerful your imagined experiences can be, but you also must become aware of the power of words. We hold private conversations with ourselves all day and most of us never stop to really listen to what we are saying. Some of our self-talk is as harmless as reminding ourselves over and over not to forget bread on the way home from school. At other times our messages may be as harmful as telling ourselves that we will NEVER be able to succeed. Try to track over a one-day period as much of your self-talk as possible by writing it down. Then discuss in class what types of things you are presently saying to yourself, and what more positive statements you should get into the habit of saying. Most of us will be surprised, if we honestly write down what we say to ourselves, how many negative messages we give ourselves every day, 365 days a year. Many of us say things to ourselves that we would never allow anyone else to say to us. If you would not allow anyone else to say it to you, then don't say it to yourself.

How do you replace your negative attitudes and self-talk? By copying over them with messages that will help you succeed. Write out two positive self-talk statements that tie in with your goals, using your name and the present tense. For example, if one of your long-term goals is to lose weight and get down to 135 lbs., then one of your positive self-talk statements could be "I, Sally Johnson, now weigh one hundred thirty-five pounds. I have lots of energy and only crave foods that are good for my body." After you have written your two statements, say them out loud to yourself with LOTS of enthusiasm a minimum of three times first thing when you wake up and right before you go to sleep. The reason for saying your statements at these times is that they are when your mind is the most open to suggestions. You must maintain this schedule for a minimum of 21 days before you will see any results. It takes the mind at least 21 days of repeated messages before it starts acting on its new information. If you are having trouble writing positive self-affirmations, look at the ones at the top of each personal comment sheet and individualize them to fit your goals.

Positive Talk with Others

In addition to using positive self-talk, you should also become more aware of how you talk with others. If you are constantly telling your instructors "I never was good at math," then you are sending a message to your brain that says "NO GOOD AT MATH." Instead, you should say, "In the past I had a problem with math, but I'm sure if you explain it to me I'll be able to learn it." Also, throw out of your vocabulary the words "wish," "hope," and "maybe." These are passive words that tell your brain that what happens to you is not in your control. For example, "I wish I could lose weight" implies there is not much you can do about it, whereas "I can lose weight" puts you back in the driver's seat.

Two more good ways to keep a positive attitude are to maintain an active sense of humor and to keep busy. Discuss in class an event that happened to you in the past that upset you at the time, but that you now see as funny. If you had laughed at it right away, the situation would have been much easier to accept.

Remember that life is a self-fulfilling prophecy. If you think life is bad, it will be; and if you think it will be good, it will be. Be prepared to discuss both of these concepts in class.

Changing for the Better

We said at the very beginning of this chapter that changing your attitudes would take some time. However, don't get discouraged. You are in the perfect situation to make these changes come about.

A Change in Environment

A good time to change is when we change our environment. If you were considered a poor student in school before, that need not affect you now. Take advantage of the fact that you are starting off with a clean slate because few people, if any, know you or will have any reason not to believe your new image. A good example of this can be found at most local video stores. In the movie *Working Girl* the main character changed her appearance when she decided to pretend to be her boss.

A Change in Appearance

By changing your appearance to one that is more professional, by starting to talk and act as if you are a good student, you will find that people will start treating you differently. Of course, you have to be willing to put in whatever time and effort is required to actually become a good student. This is an important concept because throughout life we are given a chance to start over, whether it be because of starting college, a new job, or a move to a new city. People don't know us and we have the chance to change, but many times we don't take advantage of these situations. Instead, we drag our old image along with us.

A Change to Self-Reliance

You've taken advantage of your new success-oriented environment. You've changed your appearance so that your new positive

Creating Your Own Success

attitude shows. But there is one more important change you must make. You must erase a message from your mind.

Why is it so important that you do this? Many of us have subconsciously accepted this message over time and it does more damage to our chances for success than almost any other negative message. What are we asking you to erase? — the idea that things that are worthwhile come free or at little cost in terms of effort or money. This is most people's worst problem; they are waiting for someone, anyone, to take responsibility for their life and happiness.

People hold onto the childlike hope that somehow everything will turn out all right without much effort on their part. We have almost all gotten depressed and fantasized about winning the lottery, even if we never buy tickets, or having some mysterious rich relative leave us lots of money, but this form of daydreaming is just a waste of time. We must get rid of the hope that something or someone is going to ride up on the horizon and save the day. Take control of your own destiny and accept that if it is going to happen YOU have to make it happen. Start thinking of yourself in terms of self-reliance.

What If I Fail?

How you handle failure will play a big part in whether you succeed. Sometimes people fail because it is more comfortable. They have failed before. Their families may even expect, and in a way encourage, failure. These people halfheartedly go after their goals and if they fail, they pretend that they really didn't try that hard to reach them. How many times have you heard somebody say, "I never studied for that test, and who cares about this class anyway, it's boring" after they got a low grade? If you really want to be successful, you can't cover up your failures by pretending that you don't care or by giving a half-hearted effort. You have to be willing to work as hard as you can and accept the fact that even with all your effort the outcome may not be what you wanted. You may fail. Successful people fail probably more than we do because they expose themselves to failure more. They don't try to protect themselves from failure or looking foolish.

Don't Give Up

Successful people are not quitters. A good example is Thomas Alva Edison, inventor of the light bulb. Mr. Edison performed 10,000 experiments before he developed the light bulb. Mr. Edison probably did not look at the 9,999 previous experiments as failures, but instead in his mind they were steps leading to the one that would light up the world. Would you have given up after ten experiments or maybe after one hundred? He believed in his idea and himself so strongly that he never gave up until he succeeded. Edison had a single-minded purpose to invent the light bulb. These are the kinds of stories that you can research to build up your story file and help keep yourself motivated.

We have all heard that Babe Ruth was one of the all-time great home run hitters, but most of you may not know why. He was also the holder of the record for the most strikeouts. Ruth batted a total of 8,399 times during his 22 years in the majors. Out of these 8,399 bats, he hit 714 home runs and struck out 1,330 times. This means that he hit home runs only 8.5% of the time, and struck out 15.8% of the time. He knew that you can't hit the ball if you're afraid to swing the bat. Jim Abbott, a pitcher with the New York Yankees baseball team, did not let the fact that he has only one hand stop him. He dreamed of becoming a major league pitcher and was willing to put in the effort to reach that goal. How many people do you think told him this was an impossible dream? How many do you think even laughed? Just like all winners, Jim understood that winners practice winning. Just like they practice pitching, typing, balancing a ledger, or rebuilding an engine, they are willing to accept failure as a small part of the big picture of success. Knowing that each time they practice and fail, they have learned a little more from the experience that will help them next time puts failure into proper perspective. The only way failure can prevent you from reaching your goals is if you give up on yourself.

To help you put failure in its proper perspective, ask yourself, "If I fail what is the worst thing that could happen?" You have nothing to lose especially if you can take action that will give you other options if the worst should happen. For example, you can go through this school pretending that you don't care that much about graduating or getting a new career, and get average or poor grades. On the other hand, you can admit to yourself that this is really important to your future and decide to give your very best effort every day. By doing the best you can every day, you will probably get better grades and they certainly won't be any worse than if you give it a halfway effort. You have nothing to lose and everything to gain!

Tim Giago, an Oglala Sioux, is founding editor of a newspaper named the *Indian Country Times,* formerly the *Lakota Times.* The newspaper, which was founded with a $4,000 loan from a friend, has grown into the largest American Indian newspaper. Did connections or luck allow him to realize his goal? No, it was simple hard work and the willingness to be ready when opportunity knocked. The first issue of the *Lakota Times* was printed on a borrowed press and given out for free. Now it has subscribers in all fifty states and many foreign countries. All because one man was willing to believe in himself and his dream. Just like Thomas Edison and Jim Abbott, Tim Giago was willing to work to see his vision come alive.

Bring to class one additional success story of a person who overcame his or her situation to reach a goal.

Chapter 5

More Steps On My Road To Success
A Personal Review

1. What were the key concepts discussed about attitudes?

2. How do I plan to put my new positive attitude skills into effect?

3. What are the areas I don't understand or need more information on?

4. What is my game plan for getting the additional information I need?

5. What positive changes do I see in myself?

Chapter 5 Attitudes

Exercise 1

Be prepared to discuss in class how you plan to use the following statements to help you reach your goals. Space has been provided for your response to each statement.

1. Failure is just a learning process.

2. When I fail I have a chance to try new ideas.

3. People do not remember how many times you fail, only how many times you succeed.

4. I do not compete against other people and will not allow anyone to make me feel like a failure.

5. When I fail in the future, I will first go over why I did as well as I did and then build on what I did right. Next, I will ask myself what steps I could have taken to do better.

Write your own success motto and share it with the group during the next class meeting.

Creating Your Own Success

Chapter 5 Attitudes

Exercise 2

Use this exercise as an Attitude work sheet. Place a check mark next to the ones for which you feel you need an attitude adjustment. Then under each one marked, list ways for changing your attitude.

1. _____ Family

_____
_____
_____
_____

2. _____ Friends

_____
_____
_____
_____

3. _____ You

_____
_____
_____
_____

4. _____ Your classes

_____
_____
_____
_____

5. _____ Your instructors

_____
_____
_____
_____

6. _____ Your job

_____
_____
_____
_____

7. _____ Your boss

_____
_____
_____
_____

8. _____ Other important areas

_____
_____
_____
_____

Chapter 5 Attitudes

Exercise 3

1. In an effort to help you see yourself realistically, have one of your positive success network teamates describe how they see you in terms of appearance and personality. Write down exactly what they say.

   _____
   _____
   _____
   _____

2. Ask someone you just met to do the same exercise.

   _____
   _____
   _____
   _____

3. How do their views of you differ from your view of yourself, and how can you change your attitudes so that your view of yourself is more accurate?

   _____
   _____
   _____
   _____

Chapter 5 Attitudes

Exercise 4

1. Describe how someone else's expectations of you have helped you.

   _____
   _____
   _____
   _____

2. Describe how you have allowed others' expectations to hold you back.

   _____
   _____
   _____
   _____

3. What can you learn from these two stories?

   _____
   _____
   _____
   _____

Chapter 5 Attitudes

Exercise 5

A. In this exercise you will first list the short-term goals you set for yourself in Chapter 2. Next, list how your attitudes are helping or hampering your progress towards those goals.

Short-Term Goals

Attitudes

Positive   Negative

1. _____   _____   _____
2. _____   _____   _____
3. _____   _____   _____
4. _____   _____   _____
5. _____   _____   _____

B. Now that I have listed the attitudes that are hurting my progress, I need to develop more positive attitudes I can work on replacing them with.

Negative   **Positive Replacement**

_____   _____
_____   _____
_____   _____
_____   _____
_____   _____
_____   _____
_____   _____
_____   _____
_____   _____

Chapter 5 Attitudes
Exercise 6

1. List the areas in which you need to be more self-reliant.

2. Winners practice WINNING — I am going to practice winning by doing the following success exercises:

    For example: I will practice my speaking success by answering more questions in class. I will exercise my leadership success by running for office in student council.

Case Study

This Is Your Life: Mei-Yu Liang

Mei-Yu Liang started school to please her parents and because deep down she knew it was the only way for her to get an accounting job, which has always been her dream. She is the first in her family to go to college, and though her parents are supportive, her grandparents feel she should go directly into the small family business. Reminded repeatedly by her grandfather that if she fails she can always come home where she belongs and pressured by her mother to keep at least a B average, Mei-Yu is afraid to let either side down. After two months of school, she is finding it hard to keep up with all of her classes and has received C's and D's on several assignments. When her instructors try to help, she laughs and tells them she is learning all she needs to know to run a small specialty store. Whenever her parents or grandparents ask how she's doing, Mei-Yu always shrugs and tells them the classes are boring and the instructors hard to get along with.

1. What is Mei-Yu's self-fulfilling prophecy?

2. How is she letting her family affect her success?

3. How should she handle her fear of failure so that it does not hamper her growth?

Suggested Resource Material

Books: Additional Resources

Whitman, Ardis. "Secrets of Survivors," *Readers Digest,* July 1989, pgs. 113–116.

Armbrister, Thomas. "Return of Marie Balter," *Readers Digest,* July 1989, pgs. 123–127.

Waitely, Dennis. *Seeds of Greatness.* Pocket Books Publishing Co., 1988.

Bloomfield, Harold H., M.D., & Kory, Robert. *Inner Joy.* Jove Books Publishing Co., 1985.

Carnegie, Dale. *How to Stop Worrying & Start Living.* Pocket Books Publishing Co., 1984.

Burns, David D. *Feeling Good.* NAL-Dutton-Publishing Co., 1981.

James, Muriel. *It's Never Too Late to Be Happy.* Addison-Wesley Publishing Co., 1986.

Viscott, David. *Feel Free.* Pocket Books Publishing Co., 1988.

Flach, Frederic. *Resilience.* Fawcett Books Publishing Co., 1989.

Freeman, Dr. Arthur, & DeWolf, Rose. *Woulda, Coulda, Shoulda— Overcoming Regrets, Mistakes, & Missed Opportunities.* Silver Arrow Books/Morrow Publishing Co., 1989.

Russianoff, Penelope, Ph.D. *When Am I Going to Be Happy?* Bantam Books Publishing Co., 1988.

Stone, W. E. Clement. *Success Through a Positive Mental Attitude.* Pocket Books Publishing Co., 1985.

Peale, Norman Vincent. *The Tough Minded Optimist.* Fawcett Books Publishing Co., 1986.

Chapter 6

Time Management

"I will treat my time as my most valuable resource."

Personal Comment Sheet

Entry Date _____

Five self-positives:

1. _____

2. _____

3. _____

4. _____

5. _____

Getting Focused

How do I think the information I am about to read will help me reach my goals?

_____
_____
_____
_____
_____
_____

Have you ever said to yourself, "I just don't have the time to get everything finished, or do all the things I want to do"? Not being able to manage time is frustrating. Learning to control and effectively use your time will help you face the commitment that you have made to get an education. When you first start classes, you may feel that you will be in school forever; learning about time management will help you realize that school will actually take up only a small amount of your life. Time management does not mean restrictions and someone watching you every minute. This section of the class will help you to realize that time management is not a curse but a blessing.

Figure 6-1

Time is a valuable commodity.

Time is a valuable resource and, like any other resource, we must not misuse it if we want it to work for us. Unlike other resources, time cannot be replaced or saved. You can't feel it, smell it, or taste it; it is the most elusive of all resources. Because it is so elusive it is very easy to run out of, and when you are out of it — that's it, it's gone.

Time is not prejudiced and doesn't care who uses it. Whether we are old, young, rich, or poor, we all get the same amount of time in a day to use any way we like. Use it wisely or throw it away; enjoy it or see it as a burden — no matter what happened during the last hour you just spent, you can't change it, can you? One of our goals during this section is to help you see time as the valuable commodity that it is. There are 168 hours in a week for you to divide up during your time-management projects. If you go to school 30 hours a week, work 25 hours, and sleep 56 hours, then that leaves 57 hours for homework, family, etc. One of the key lessons that we need to learn about time management is that if you schedule 180 hours of projects a week, no matter how good you are, you are bound to fail and feel frustrated.

Basic Time-Management Principles

Stop. Before you read any further take a second to think about how you use your time. In the margin of this page or in your notes, make a quick list of your time-wasting habits. Now as you read the following principles place a star next to the ones that you need to concentrate on. Put a paper clip or turn back the corners of these pages and refer to them daily until these positive time-management principles become second nature.

96 Creating Your Own Success

Figure Out What Time of Day You're at Your Best

Each person has a peak period of energy sometime during the day when he or she is most productive. Figure out what times of day your peak periods are and do those things on which you want to do your best work during these peak times. You will find that during these times your production will be twice as high. For some people the early morning hours are peak times and "early morning" means 4 a.m. This may seem ridiculous, but early morning is a wonderful time because the world is quiet and you are free of all the inner clutter that the rest of the day brings. The mind is better able to focus — no telephones, or traffic jams, or lost parking places. Try this technique and see if it works for you by scheduling study time for the early morning. Who knows — you might even see a beautiful sunrise. If you find that you are not an early morning person, try other times. You may find that you really pick up steam in the mid-afternoon or early evening. It doesn't make any difference which time works best for you. Just be aware of your peak energy flow and plan to use this time to your advantage.

Schedule Difficult or Boring Things First

Doing the difficult or least stimulating things first will insure their completion while you are still fresh. With these things behind you, the rest of your work will seem easier. If you do the things you like best first, whether they are high priority or not, you may run out of energy before the difficult things are completed.

Plan Enough Time for Each Task

Trying to cram everything you must do into a short amount of time will not assure you of success, but instead will keep you from doing your best. This is especially true of study time. For some subjects, you may need to schedule at least two hours of study time for every hour spent in class. Avoid long study sessions by planning to break them up into three or four 2-hour sessions instead of one 10-hour session. You will be more productive.

Use Waiting Time to Your Advantage

If you must wait 20 or 30 minutes for a bus or at the doctor's office, use this time to catch up on reading assignments. The laundromat is also an excellent place to use waiting time. Use it to catch up on letter writing or reading. If you find it difficult to concentrate on reading new material while you are waiting, use this time for review. By using either your class notes or three-by-five summary cards listing possible test questions, key terms, and ideas, you can use the time to lock information deeper into your brain. This will be covered in more detail in Chapter 7. One advantage to using three-by-five cards is that by slipping them into your pocket or purse, they are always available. Waiting time doesn't have to be wasted time, so make use of it.

Figure 6-2

Summary cards can turn wasted time into study time.

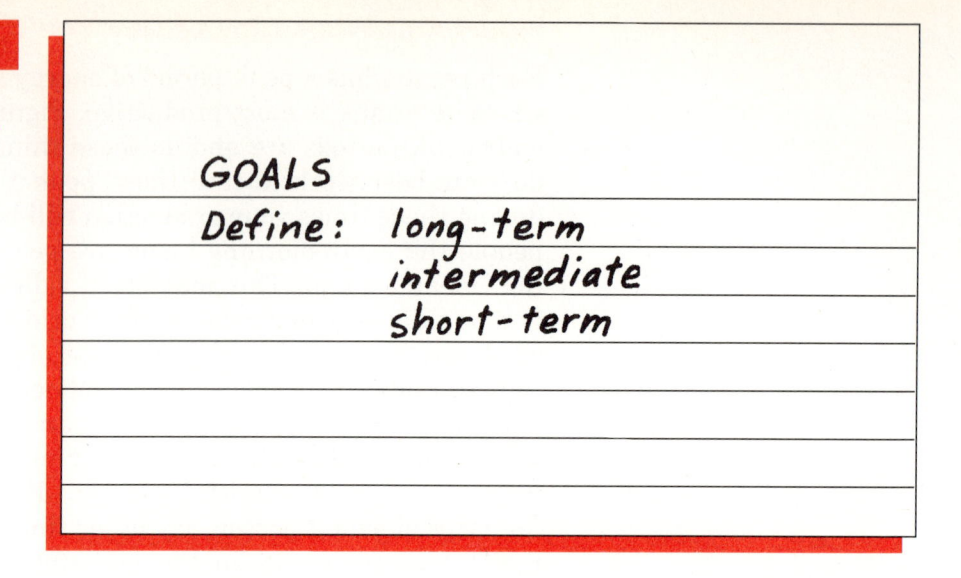

> GOALS
> Define: long-term
>   intermediate
>   short-term

Study in a Planned Area

Cut out as much interference as possible. Every time you are interrupted, it takes time to gear out of what you are doing and then gear back up again. Having a regular study area is also valuable psychologically because you are prepared to study whenever you are in this area. Training your mind by having a regular study area is the same as preparing your mind for sleep when you recline on the bed or to snack when you are in the kitchen. If you are where you can hear the TV, your mind will wander away from what you are doing and you will find yourself listening to the TV. The same thing applies to the radio. Studying burns calories, which is another good reason to be actively involved in studying. Remember, being too comfortable undermines your concentration. The library is a perfect place to study because it is designed with that in mind. It's quiet and gives the brain a chance to take over and calm the body.

Learn to Say "No"

People often do not realize how much time is used in idle conversation on the telephone. It is very hard to tell a friend, "I'm sorry, but I'm very busy right now. May I call you back on Sunday?" But if you value your time, you must learn to do so. Friends and family sometimes just take it for granted that you will run and pick up Susie or Johnny. Learning to say no is hard, but friends that are really friends will understand that you are doing something right now that means a lot to you. Be aware of how others are misusing your time and learn to say no. If someone calls or drops by when you are studying, explain at the beginning of the conversation that you are in the middle of a study period, and though you are glad they called or stopped by, you will have to get together or chat at another time.

Schedule Time for Relaxation

All work and no play will contribute to burnout, which will be discussed more thoroughly in Chapter 12. Be good to yourself and reward yourself with time to do just what you want to do. Taking a break every now and then is vital to your health and well-being.

Work Until You Are Finished

You will find an increase in your productivity if you ask yourself at the end of a long day to do just one more short task. It takes conditioning to make the most of your time.

Work as If You Were Being Paid

If you were self-employed, would you be earning your wages? Using your time wisely is a self-investment. If you are wasting it, then you are wasting yourself. Do not feel that you are accomplishing something just because you are busy. The goal of time management is to work smart, not just hard. Look at how you work and figure out ways that you can work smart. For example, if you have assignments in math, English, and accounting, schedule your homework time so that you do the math and accounting back to back. You will already have your pencils, calculators, and brain ready to deal with numbers. Then do your English homework.

Get Family Support

Have a family meeting and discuss what you are doing and how it will benefit everyone in the end. Their support and understanding will help you succeed. If you cannot gain their support, make sure that you build a strong support network at school.

Write Down Your Time-Wasting Habits

- Do you spend too much time on the phone?
- Do you spend a lot of time in front of the TV?
- Do you often sleep late?
- Do you take more time than is needed to finish simple tasks?
- Do you do just one thing at a time?
- Do you take a lot of extra breaks during the day?

Write down all the time-wasting habits you have and post them in your study area where you can look at them each time you sit down. At the bottom of your list write in big bold letters: I VALUE MY TIME AND USE IT WISELY. When you have given up all the time-wasters on your list, you will be able to see it was all worth it.

Take Occasional Goal Breaks

If you catch your mind wandering during study time, take a GOAL BREAK. Get out your goal sheets and Goal Board from

Chapter 2 and recommit your energies to reaching them. Focus all of your imagination on what life will feel like when you have reached your goals. Then turn your complete attention back to the work that will help you get there.

Learn to Delegate

Take a look at all of your activities and see if there are some you can delegate. Are your children old enough to start picking up their own areas? Can you join with other students to form a study group in which each individual is assigned a class you all have in common, develops study questions, and then reviews with the rest of the team? Can you and a friend switch babysitting duties so you both get four hours a week of uninterrupted study time?

Group Your "To Do's"

Learn to group common "to do's." If you have several written assignments, then write all of your rough outlines first. Next, make a list of all of the areas you need additional information on and go to the library to look for answers to these questions. Then wait until you've written all of the assignments to sit down with the dictionary and check the spelling. By grouping your work, you save trips, are more organized both mentally and physically, and since many of your classes are related you will begin to see how all of your subjects tie together. For example, if you are writing a short essay on solid accounting principles and another on starting your own small business, you will see how basic accounting knowledge is essential to the survival of new businesses.

Deal Calmly with a Crisis

If you have a crisis in your life, and almost everyone does at one time or another, the first thing to remember is not to panic. It's true that a crisis will add more stress, usually just in the short term, and may make it seem impossible to complete the things on your "to do" list, or even worse to reach your goals. After you remember not to panic, do the following things:

- Look at your "to do" list and draw a line through any priority less than a "B." You can always pick these items up later.

Figure 6-3

Don't be afraid to seek help when a crisis arises.

- Contact your success network support team and discuss how they can assist you during this crisis period.

- This is no time to be brave. Let those who care about your success help. Talk with your instructors, school counselors, and school administrators. Explain what is happening in your life and why you are feeling a time or emotional crunch.

- Review your goals more frequently than you normally do. If you feel your stress level rising, get your Goal Board out and stare at it while reminding yourself that you have the power to reach your goals.

- For the short term be willing to settle for less than your best rather than giving up. During this crisis period, your attendance may suffer and your attitude may even take a blow or two, but if you have let your instructors, administrators, and success network team know what's going on, you will find the strength you need. It's true that employers look for people with good grades and attendance. But it is also true that they are impressed with people who have faced adversity with determination.

- Remember that no matter how tough things may seem now, one thing life ensures all of us is change. As the saying goes, "This too shall pass."

- Decide now that you will NEVER give up.

Figure 6-4

Time
For Better or Worse

We have but one life to live,
and time is the element we are given to make it worthwhile.
We can waste it and wish for more than our allotted amount,
Or we can use it wisely and make every minute count.

by
V. Rose Kitchen

Chapter 6   Time Management   101

Time-Management Tools

Doug Whitehorse has decided to follow all of the basic time-management principles. By doing his most difficult work first, turning off the TV during study time, and grouping his "to do's," he has increased his grades to all B's. But he is still having trouble keeping track of his time and deciding which work to do first. Instead of getting frustrated, he meets with his instructor and asks for help. Praising his progress, Mrs. Kisner hands him a packet and promises that the enclosed forms will work "magic."

How can she make such a promise? Because she knows that when Doug fills out the time-management forms she gave him it will force him to choose how he uses his time. Without following a basic format, it is too easy for us, just like Doug, to lose track of both how we spend our time and what we have to do.

The following forms will help you see how you use your time, and help you set priorities, organize projects, and make decisions. But just like any of the other tools we have shared with you, they only work if you use them.

Time Tracker

Wise time management is like wise money management. To make the most of what you have, sometimes a good working budget is necessary. If you are on a limited income then you know the importance of every penny. The same rules apply to time; being aware of how you spend every minute can help you be more productive.

Before you can design a budget that works, it's necessary to track the time you use. This will give you a clear picture of how you spend your time.

What is a Time Tracker? It is simply a form that breaks the hours in a day down into 30-minute segments. Next to each of these segments is a line for you to write down what you did during that time period. See Figure 6-5 for an example of this form.

The purpose of tracking your time is to allow you to see how you use it. For this to be an effective tool, you must be honest. If you just spent the last half hour talking with cousin Susan about what a witch Aunt Bertha is, even if your math book happened to be lying open in front of you, you can't enter that you were studying math. If you choose to be less than honest on this form, you are only cheating yourself.

All right, you've been honest and written down exactly how you spent your time for the last seven days. Now what? By tallying up how you used your time, you can more easily pick out both your peak periods and time-wasting habits. As you look over the days, do you find most of your work happening in the morning? This would indicate that you peak during this time. Do you spot a block of time every day spent on the phone to friends when you should be studying? With this knowledge you can reschedule these chats so they don't interfere with your study time.

Table 6-1

Time Tracker

Time Tracker

Monday/Date __11/4__

AM
- 7:00 shower & breakfast
- 7:30 dressed & headed for school
- 8:00 another cup of coffee, went over class work
- 8:30 attended first hour class
- 9:00 9:20 — ten min. break — personal time
- 9:30 second hour class
- 10:00 10:20 break, finished class notes
- 10:30 third hour class
- 11:00
- 11:30 had lunch and went to the library
- 12:00 had planned to study, visited w/classmate instead

PM
- 12:30 fourth hour class
- 1:00 1:20, break time, stayed in typing
- 1:30 fifth hour class
- 2:00
- 2:30 got something to drink and filled car w/gas
- 3:00 got ready to work
- 3:30 work
- 4:00 work
- 4:30 work
- 5:00 break & back to work
- 5:30 work
- 6:00 work
- 6:30 work
- 7:00 work
- 7:30 home/fix dinner
- 8:00 spent time with family and relaxed
- 8:30 family time
- 9:00 started homework
- 9:30
- 10:00

Total hours I feel good about __14½__
Total hours I goofed off __½__

Chapter 6 — Time Management

Calendar

If you can't remember what you have to do, you cannot use your time effectively. A calendar can do wonders for keeping your time and tasks organized. Use your calendar to record meetings, test dates, due dates of homework assignments, and anything else that requires a specific time frame or deadline.

What kind of calendar should you buy? When you look at the selection at your local office supply store, it may be tempting to pick up the fancy leather-bound agenda. Unless you just feel like splurging, it is not necessary. Any calendar will do as long as it has enough space for each day so that you can list your "to do's."

Success Schedule

A "to do" list helps you keep track of all of the things you must accomplish in the next seven days. At the beginning of each week write down everything you need to do. Do not worry about writing them down in any particular order. After you have listed each item, start at the top of the list and mark each one with an A, B, C, or D, with A being the highest priority item and D being the lowest. As you complete each task, mark it off with a check mark.

Table 6-2

Success Schedule

Success Schedule

Things to Do List — Priority List — A, B, C, D

1. study Geography notes (test Thurs.) * B
2. organize record albums * D
3. math homework due tomorrow ✓ * A
4. read Chapter 6 data-processing * A
5. pick up laundry * C
6. return calculator to Mike * B
7. financial aid appointment ✓ * A
8. return books to library * B
9. ___ *
10. ___ *
11. ___ *
12. ___ *
13. ___ *
14. ___ *
15. ___ *
16. ___ *
17. ___ *

At the end of the week transfer any "to do's" that didn't get done to next week's sheet. If you keep transferring the same C's and D's, then take a second to decide whether they even need to be on your list. Also as you make this transfer, decide if the letter designation you gave the "to do" still applies. For example, you promised to speak at the next orientation. As you copy your "to do" list four weeks before the date, writing a speech might be a C. By the week before the event, the same task would have moved up to an A.

Project Tracker

Have you ever received an assignment and just had no idea where to start? You're not alone. Many of us have felt this way. But a Project Tracker can help end this problem. Its purpose is to help you list all of the steps that must be completed to finish a project on time. This form helps you think about each step, giving it a deadline for completion so that you do not find yourself "deadlining" your work or missing turning in projects altogether.

Table 6-3

Project Tracker

Project Tracker

Project: Five-page paper: "Role Models of This Century"
Due Date: Three Weeks — Sept. 13th
Class: Communications 103
Instructor: Ms. Tuteria

To Do	Due Date Strategy	Completed
Develop list of 4 people	Aug. 26, library	✓
1st rough draft	Sept. 1, organize notes	✓
	type outline	✓

The Decision Maker

Each time you allocate your time you must make a decision. Some of these are clear cut, but most choices have both pros and cons. The following method of making wise decisions has been credited to Benjamin Franklin, but no matter who first thought of it, it is a very effective tool. The basic concept is that rather than just thinking about a decision, problem, or concern that you face, you must define the situation by writing it down and listing the pluses and minuses.

How do you get started? A Decision Maker is simply a piece of paper with a line down the middle. On the left side you enter the pros and on the right side you enter the cons.

Let's work through an example for Bill, a twenty-five-year-old man who is forty pounds overweight. Trying to decide whether he should go to the effort to lose the extra pounds, he grabs a Decision Maker form and begins to write.

With nine strong Pros it's pretty easy to see what Bill has decided. After he enters his decision, he should recopy this list of Pros and tape it to the refrigerator door for extra motivation.

Table 6-4

Decision Maker

Decision Maker

Define decision, problem, or concern: *I am afraid my weight will hurt my chance of getting a good job.*

Pros to: *Losing weight*   Cons:

1. *Feel better about myself*
2. *Clothes would fit better*
3. *Should have more energy*
4. *Longer life*
5. *More attractive*
6. *Less health problems*
7. *Could play basketball again*
8. *Would look younger*
9. *Need new clothes for work, best time to change*

1. *Hate exercise*
2. *Have to cut calories*
3. *Might get hungry*
4. *Give up fried foods*
5. *Would need new clothes*
6.
7.
8.
9.

My decision: _____

Creating Your Own Success

Chapter 6

More Steps On My Road To Success
A Personal Review

1. What were the key concepts discussed about time management?

2. How do I plan to put this new time-management knowledge into effect?

3. What are the areas I don't understand or need more information on?

4. What is my game plan for getting the additional information I need?

5. What positive changes do I see in myself?

Chapter 6   Time Management

Exercise 1

Use the following Time Tracker to keep an accurate account of your daily activities for an entire week. "To thine own self be true," and make the Time Tracker work for your benefit. At the end of the week, count the hours spent productively and the hours spent unproductively. Expect to be surprised at how much time is spent unproductively.

Don't be too hard on yourself. Nearly everyone is guilty at one time or another of wasting time. The bright side is that you have taken the first step in gaining control of your time.

When you have completed the Time Tracker for one week, count up the hours you have spent productively. Make sure your hours do not total more than 168 (7 days x 24 hours). Be prepared to discuss in class how this exercise worked for you.

Time Tracker

Monday/Date _____

AM

7:00 _____

7:30 _____

8:00 _____

8:30 _____

9:00 _____

9:30 _____

10:00 _____

10:30 _____

11:00 _____

11:30 _____

12:00 _____

PM

12:30 _____

1:00 _____

1:30 _____

2:00 _____

2:30 _____

3:00 _____

3:30 _____

4:00 _____

4:30 _____

5:00 _____

5:30 _____

6:00 _____

6:30 _____

7:00 _____

7:30 _____

8:00 _____

8:30 _____

9:00 _____

9:30 _____

10:00 _____

Total hours I feel good about _____

Total hours I goofed off _____

Tuesday/Date _____

AM

   7:00 _____

   7:30 _____

   8:00 _____

8:30 _____
9:00 _____
9:30 _____
10:00 _____
10:30 _____
11:00 _____
11:30 _____
12:00 _____

PM

12:30 _____
1:00 _____
1:30 _____
2:00 _____
2:30 _____
3:00 _____
3:30 _____
4:00 _____
4:30 _____
5:00 _____
5:30 _____
6:00 _____
6:30 _____
7:00 _____
7:30 _____
8:00 _____
8:30 _____
9:00 _____

9:30 _____

10:00 _____

Total hours I feel good about _____

Total hours I goofed off _____

Wednesday/Date

AM

7:00 _____

7:30 _____

8:00 _____

8:30 _____

9:00 _____

9:30 _____

10:00 _____

10:30 _____

11:00 _____

11:30 _____

12:00 _____

PM

12:30 _____

1:00 _____

1:30 _____

2:00 _____

2:30 _____

3:00 _____

3:30 _____

4:00 _____

4:30 _____

5:00 _____

5:30 _____

6:00 _____

6:30 _____

7:00 _____

7:30 _____

8:00 _____

8:30 _____

9:00 _____

9:30 _____

10:00 _____

Total hours I feel good about _____

Total hours I goofed off _____

Thursday/Date _____

AM

7:00 _____

7:30 _____

8:00 _____

8:30 _____

9:00 _____

9:30 _____

10:00 _____

10:30 _____

11:00 _____

11:30 _____

112   **Creating Your Own Success**

12:00 _____
PM   _____
12:30 _____
1:00 _____
1:30 _____
2:00 _____
2:30 _____
3:00 _____
3:30 _____
4:00 _____
4:30 _____
5:00 _____
5:30 _____
6:00 _____
6:30 _____
7:00 _____
7:30 _____
8:00 _____
8:30 _____
9:00 _____
9:30 _____
10:00 _____

Total hours I feel good about _____

Total hours I goofed off _____

Friday/Date _____

AM

7:00 _____

7:30 _____

8:00 _____

8:30 _____

9:00 _____

9:30 _____

10:00 _____

10:30 _____

11:00 _____

11:30 _____

12:00 _____

PM

12:30 _____

1:00 _____

1:30 _____

2:00 _____

2:30 _____

3:00 _____

3:30 _____

4:00 _____

4:30 _____

5:00 _____

5:30 _____

6:00 _____

6:30 _____

7:00 _____

7:30 _____

8:00 _____

8:30 _____

9:00 _____

9:30 _____

10:00 _____

Total hours I feel good about _____

Total hours I goofed off _____

Chapter 6   Time Management

Exercise 2

Use the following "to do" list to enter all of the different things you need to accomplish in the next seven days. At the end of the seven-day period, be prepared to discuss in class how this time-management tool worked for you. P.S.: Don't expect miracles. At first, using these time-management tools will feel awkward, and maybe even restrictive. As we discussed in the Attitudes chapter, Winners Practice Winning. Practicing good time-management techniques until they feel natural is part of the package.

Success Schedule

Things to Do List   **Priority list - A, B, C, D**

1. _____   *
2. _____   *
3. _____   *
4. _____   *
5. _____   *
6. _____   *
7. _____   *
8. _____   *
9. _____   *
10. _____   *
11. _____   *
12. _____   *
13. _____   *
14. _____   *
15. _____   *
16. _____   *

Creating Your Own Success

Chapter 6   Time Management

Exercise 3

For practice complete this form, showing all the steps you would need to take to successfully complete a five-page report, due in three weeks, on "Role Models of This Century."

Project Tracker

Project: Five-page paper — "Role Models of This Century"
Due Date: Three weeks — Sept. 13th
Class: Communications 103
Instructor: Ms. Tuteria

To Do	Due Date Strategy	Completed
Develop list of four people	Aug. 26, library	✓
1st rough draft	Sept. 1, organize notes	✓

Chapter 6 Time Management

Exercise 4

Now it's your turn to use the Decision Maker. Fill out the following form to help you make a decision or reconfirm a decision you have already made.

Decision Maker

Define decision, problem, or concern: _____
_____

Pros to: _____ **Cons:**

1. _____ 1. _____
2. _____ 2. _____
3. _____ 3. _____
4. _____ 4. _____
5. _____ 5. _____
6. _____ 6. _____
7. _____ 7. _____
8. _____ 8. _____
9. _____ 9. _____
10. _____ 10. _____

My decision: _____
_____
_____

Creating Your Own Success

Chapter 6 Time Management

Exercise 5

1. My peak period is _____

2. Describe where you study most of the time.

3. My time wasting habits are:

4. I am going to group the following upcoming "to do's" so I maximize my time.

5. I need to discuss the importance of my scheduled study times with the following friends or family members so they will understand when I say no.

6. I can delegate the following responsibilities to free up more of my time.

7. What regular waiting times do I have that can be turned into review or study time?

8. The best way for me to study in the above places is to

    a. read new material.

    b. review my summary notes.

    c. study my class notes.

    d. other ideas:

Chapter 6   Time Management   119

Case Study

A Man and Three Kids

Leo, a single parent, has three children, ages six, eight, and twelve. He is going to school twenty hours a week and works part time at a temporary agency to meet expenses. His mother, a widow in her late seventies, lives next door and takes care of the children until he gets off work at 5:00 p.m., but by then she is frazzled and rushes directly back home. This leaves Leo with three wound-up kids and a minimum of two and a half hours of homework and reading.

1. How can he best schedule these evening hours to meet both his and the kids' needs?

2. If Leo were your best friend and mentioned he was thinking of dropping out, what advice would you give him, using the following Decision Maker to back up your suggestions?

120 Creating Your Own Success

Decision Maker for Leo

Define decision, problem, or concern: _____

_____

Pros to: _____   **Cons:**

1. _____   1. _____

2. _____   2. _____

3. _____   3. _____

4. _____   4. _____

5. _____   5. _____

6. _____   6. _____

7. _____   7. _____

8. _____   8. _____

9. _____   9. _____

10. _____   10. _____

My decision: _____

_____

_____

Suggested Resource Material

Books: Additional Resources

Hobbs, Charles R. *Time Power.* Harper & Collins Publishing Co., 1987.

Blanchard, Kenneth H., & Johnson, Spencer. *The One Minute Manager.* Marrow Publishing Co., 1982.

MacKenze, Alec. *The Time Trap.* Amacom Publishing Co., 1991.

Chapter 7
Memory Techniques

"The more times I input the same information the more accurate the output will be."

Personal Comment Sheet

Entry Date _____

Five self-positives:

1. _____

2. _____

3. _____

4. _____

5. _____

Getting Focused

How do I think the information I am about to read will help me reach my goals?

_____
_____
_____
_____
_____
_____

123

A good memory is a valuable tool that will help you reach your goals. A usable memory will be able to remember facts, names, dates, numbers, and of course directions. Unfortunately, there are no miracles that will help you to automatically remember information. These tips take practice and patience like all skills. You cannot expect sudden unrealistic improvement. Increasing your memory power takes time. But with attention, concentration, and practice, your memory will improve.

Figure 7-1

You can improve your memory with practice.

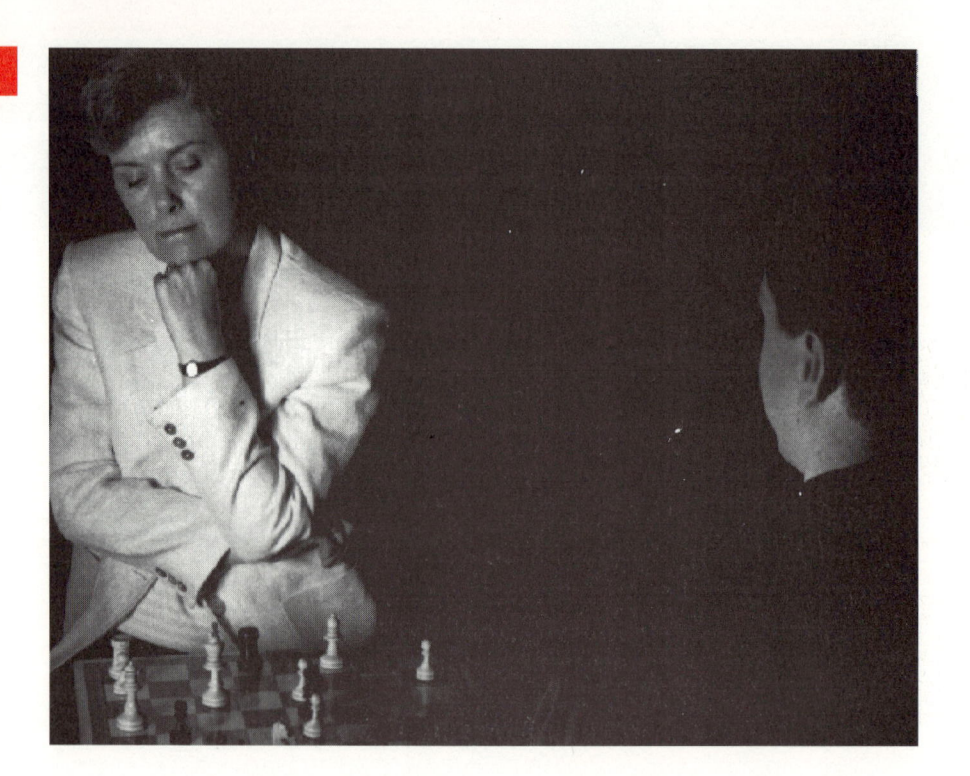

Long- and Short-term Memory

There are two kinds of memory: long-term and short-term. Short-term memory is the kind you use when you call directory assistance to find a phone number, and remember it only long enough to make the call. It is the kind of memory that has a limited capacity and only retains the information for a short time.

Long-term memory represents the kind of information you will need to recall over and over, perhaps for years. Obviously the more you recall it, the deeper it is imbedded in your brain.

A usable memory is the type of memory that enables you to recall the right information at the right time. You do not have to memorize every spoken or written word to have a usable memory.

Condition Yourself to Remember

As with every skill you must condition yourself mentally with the preparations needed to develop your memory. Examples of conditioning include: when you go to a party you are conditioned for fun; sitting down to the dinner table you are conditioned to eat; when

Creating Your Own Success

driving a car your reflexes are conditioned to respond before you even think about what is happening. It is just as important to condition yourself by preparing to remember.

Attention and Concentration Are Important

Focus your attention and cut down on any outside interference that affects your concentration. Create an atmosphere that conditions you for remembering, like a quiet study area with as little noise as possible — no TV, radio, ringing telephone, etc. The library is an excellent place. If the library isn't possible, then you must try to create this type of atmosphere somewhere else.

Memory Techniques to Use All Your Senses

Involving all of your senses can greatly improve your ability to remember. By seeing, hearing, saying, and writing material, you give your brain several chances to remember it. What are some good ways to involve your senses?

Glancing at the clock Gino turns off the TV, turns on more lights, and moves to the small card table in the corner of his studio apartment. Getting out his "to do" list, he decides to start with the first category A item, which is a reading assignment in his general business class. Skimming the material, he writes questions he wants to look for the answers to in his in-depth read. Next, he rereads the chapter carefully, taking the time to highlight the important information, find the answers to the questions from his skimming, and write additional questions in the margins of his book. After a five-minute break to stretch and get a drink of water, he turns back to the beginning of the chapter and reads it aloud while making an outline of the key ideas in his notebook. Can you spot all the ways Gino helped lock this information into his brain?

At the end of his study session Gino has seen the material three times by skimming, doing an in-depth read, and then by reading it aloud. What did Gino accomplish by reading the material aloud? Not only did he give his brain another chance to retain the information but he also involved one of his other senses. His brain was actively learning by hearing the words and seeing them again, both in the book and as he developed his outline. In addition, Gino has used several other positive study habits during our example. Can you find them?

Did Gino do everything he could to help his memory retain this information? No. There are still a few more techniques he could put into practice. While reading, he could relate the information to something he already understands. Since the chapter covered a small business balance sheet, he could compare this to his personal checking account. By thinking about how his check register works like a simple balance sheet and then figuring out how the two differ, he will have an easier time remembering the information.

But in our example, what if Gino doesn't have a checking account? Don't despair. There is another technique he can use to

Chapter 7   Memory Techniques   125

help him remember. Let's go back to his studio apartment. With his elbow leaning on the card table, he pictures himself as the vice president of a major bank, which is one of his long-term goals. Taking time to paint a detailed picture in his head, he transforms his small corner study area into a rich walnut-paneled office with a custom desk. Holding onto this vivid image, he begins to read the chapter and visualizes himself using the information in this job setting.

Now some of you may think that this kind of "pretending" is a signal that Gino is just one step away from the loony bin. But though it may sound a little silly at first, it does work. Remember what we talked about in Chapter 2 about visualization and how it can help you reach your goals? This type of visualization allows you to "shoot" a short film with you as the star and helps you use your senses to recall the information. Remember, the more vividly we send a picture to our mind, whether it involves general information or a goal affirmation, the easier it is for the brain to retrieve or act on it. If you doubt this, think about how easy it is to recall the latest gossip. Our brain can remember it because it is usually exciting and told in vivid detail. By visualizing information in this same vibrant detail, using our senses and imagination, we will find it much easier to remember. Now it's your turn. Think about one of your current reading assignments. What information do you already know that you can relate it to? How can you use visualization to help you retain it?

Organize What You Are Trying to Remember

After school you need to stop by the grocery store. Tired of getting home time after time and finding that you have forgotten something, you decide to follow Uncle Chester's sure-fire memory technique. Stopping first at the produce section, you remember that you need three things, all of which start with an "A." Happily picking up apples, asparagus, and artichokes, you finish the rest of your shopping in record time. At home you unpack the bag to find that you have remembered everything you needed and pick up the phone to thank Uncle Chester for his sage advice. Can you figure out what sure-fire memory technique he shared?

By putting the items you need to remember in groups or categories, you will find them easier to remember. Knowing that everything from the produce section started with an "A" helped you remember what you needed. And keeping in mind that you needed three things, as opposed to six or seven, was another way to trigger your memory. If you have a list of items to remember, numbering each of them and then associating the number with the item will help you recall the information.

Using the first letter of each item is not the only way you can categorize things. If in your travel and tourism geography class you needed to learn all of the states, you could do it by region — northern, southern, eastern, western, and central. Or you could choose to remember them by grouping them into their different time zones. Take a second now to think about a subject in which you have an upcoming test. Actually take the textbook out and list how you can categorize the information so it is easier to remember.

Be Repetitive

In several places in this book we have said that nothing can take the place of practice. Well, we are going to say it again. And again. And again. That's right. By reading information over, doing several of the same types of problems, and reviewing your notes at the end of the week and at least once a month, you give your brain a better chance to remember the information.

Another way to use repetition to increase your memory power is to discuss the information with others. By teaching the material to someone else, you help lock in the information and spot areas where your understanding is weak. If you are a member of a study group, take turns reviewing with each other. During these sessions discuss what you have learned and do some brainstorming about how you will use this information once you start your career. If you have children, at the end of each school day, take a few minutes to tell each other what you learned today. Your children do not have to be in school for this to be effective. By talking about what you are learning in your own words, you help strengthen your understanding of the material.

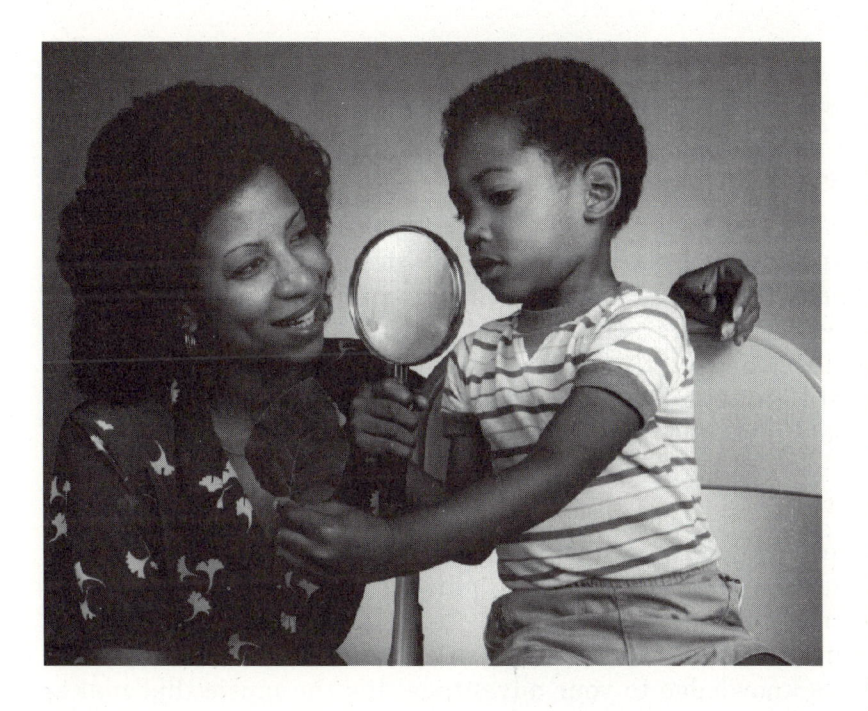

If your instructor assigns five problems out of ten, do you do the minimum required or do you work part or all of the other five? By doing more of the problems you give your mind more chances to practice retrieving the information you need. It is particularly important that you get extra practice in those areas where you are the weakest. Of course, none of us enjoys forcing ourselves to do things that are hard or confusing. But it's this type of extra effort that makes winners.

How many of you remember the children's story about the little train that said "I think I can, I think I can"? This simple story taught that you could reach your goals if you believed it was possible. This is also true with remembering information. As you study just say repeatedly in your mind, "I can remember this, I can remember this."

Figure 7-2

Repeating to another what you have learned increases your memory power.

Chapter 7   Memory Techniques   127

Be Creative

Shutting her accounting book, Demetra closes her eyes and tries to remember what she has just read. Frustrated, she begins to hum. Soon she begins to snap her fingers to the rhythm and, opening her book, makes up a silly rhyme about the entries that go on a ledger. In class the next day she reads the first question on the test and, remembering her little song, easily enters the answer.

Demetra has just used another memory method. By using associations, poems, abbreviations, songs, stories, or clustering, you can help your brain retain information.

Associations

Use associations. If you are trying to remember a name, remember someone else with the same name. For example, if the person's name you are trying to remember is Sarah, and you have a sister named Sarah, then think of your sister to recall the person's name.

Poems

Write a poem — "In 1492 Columbus sailed the blue," or "I before E except after C."

Abbreviations

In today's fast-paced world we save time when talking by using just the first initials of words. For example, try saying "Thank Goodness It's Friday." It's a lot faster to just say TGIF, isn't it? Besides being faster, this form of verbal shorthand can help you remember things. If there is a new term you have to learn, like Optical Character Reader, remember it by its initials, OCR. What other abbreviations can you think of?

Songs

How many of you can turn on your favorite radio station and sing the words to almost every song played? Being able to remember easily the words to a song and yet struggling to remember the facts in your textbooks is frustrating, isn't it? Instead of being irritated, use this knowledge to your advantage. It's the music that makes it easy for you to remember the words. A particular drum beat or series of notes from the saxophone triggers your memory as to what comes next. Just as in our example of Demetra, you can make up your own tunes to help you remember the necessary information. If you feel silly doing this, just keep in mind that this is how most of us learned our ABC's. If associating information with music worked for us then, it will work for us now.

Stories

Write a story. The following is a story written for a fifth grader to help her memorize the thirteen colonies. The story is ridiculous, but that doesn't matter; it worked.

Two beautiful white swans were swimming on a lake in (1.CONNECTICUT). Each swan wore a blue (2.DELAWARE) bell and the bells played the tune (3.GEORGIA). The tune made everyone in the area so happy it was a regular (4.MARYLAND).

A plane flew overhead and dropped a MASS-A-CHUTES. (5.MASSACHUSETTS). The Massachusetts fell on a (6.NEW HAMPSHIRE) hog and a (7.NEW JERSEY) cow. The (8.NEW YORKshire) terrier laughed so loud it could be heard in (9.NORTH CAROLINA), where they were trying to PENCIL-VAINLY (10.PENNSYLVANIA) what they heard. A (11.RHODE ISLAND) rooster fell off a fence post in (12.SOUTH CAROLINA) when a storm blew in from (13.VIRGINIA).

Try Clustering

This technique, which is also called mind mapping, allows you to be creative and build on what you already know about the subject you are getting ready to study. Start this building process by taking a blank sheet of paper and writing the name of the subject you are going to learn about in the middle of the page. After you have drawn a circle around the word, start writing down anything that comes to mind that you know about the subject. These words can be placed anywhere you like on the paper and should also have a circle around them. In addition to words, you may draw or doodle little pictures to represent what you know. During this phase make no attempt to organize the information, just write it down as it flows from your mind. As you do this you will probably be surprised at how much you already know about the subject you are getting ready to study. After five or ten minutes, stop and by using colored pens or different types of lines (dashes, wide, narrow, etc.), link together those words or pictures that belong together. For example, if you drew a cluster about goals, you might have written down *long-term, goal board, short-term, intermediate,* and *look at daily.* You would then connect the circles around the words *long-term, intermediate,* and *short-term* because these are all types of goals. Next, you would connect *goal board* and *look at daily* because these are things that help you reach your goals.

Figure 7-3

Clustering Technique

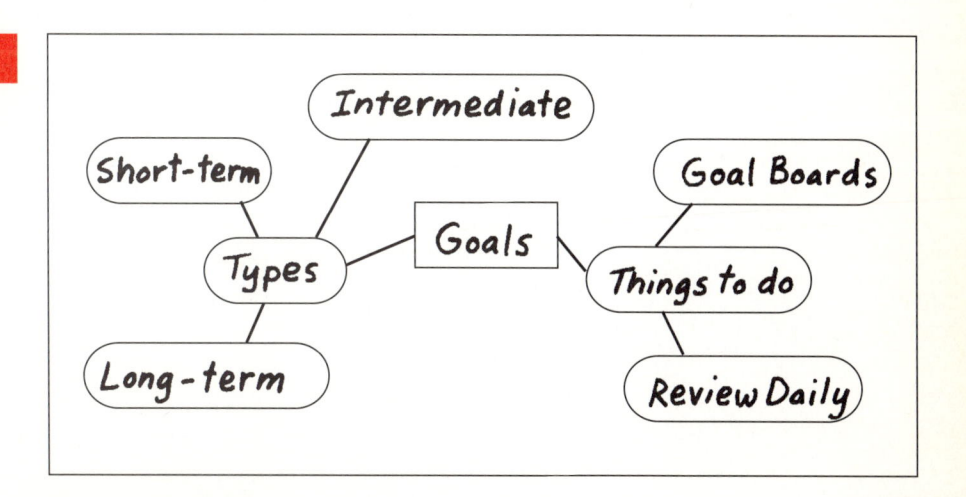

By drawing this cluster, you have not only seen how much you already know but also are getting your mind prepared to study and store what you don't know. Now it is time to begin reading by looking at chapter headings and seeing where they fit in the cluster you drew. After you finish reading, add the new information you learned to your drawing.

By creating one- or two-minute clusters from your class notes or after lectures or discussions, you will help organize the thoughts and lock them into your brain. Label these sheets and keep them as part of your notebook for study guides. Remember, not all of our brains use the same filing and retrieval methods. Clustering will help you develop a system that works best for you.

Use the above techniques separately or combine them to help in developing a usable memory. All of these techniques are useful, but there are no shortcuts for reviewing and understanding the material you are trying to memorize.

Chapter 7

More Steps On My Road To Success
A Personal Review

1. What were the key concepts discussed about memory?

2. How do I plan to put my new memory knowledge into effect?

3. What are the areas I don't understand or need more information on?

4. What is my game plan for getting the additional information I need?

5. What positive changes do I see in myself?

Chapter 7 Memory Techniques

Exercise 1

If you have several things you must memorize, putting the items into groups or categories will make them easier to remember.

Example: Try to memorize the following list of words as shown; then put the words into categories — for example, Birds, Vegetables, and Flowers. See which way is easiest for you.

robin	potato	crow
violet	cardinal	broccoli
peas	rose	petunia
canary	corn	carrot
iris	parrot	lilac

Creating Your Own Success

Chapter 7　Memory Techniques

Exercise 2

All of the words listed below relate to success. Using them, write a story, song, or poem. Don't worry if it is bizarre or ridiculous as long as it works. A blank page has been provided if you need additional writing space. Remember, the purpose is to help you memorize the words, so try to keep your story as brief as possible.

Goals	Test
Time	Success
Listening	Class
Attitude	Instructor
Memory	Friend

Exercise 2 (cont'd)

Now, without looking at your story or the list, try to write the 10 words.

1. _____   6. _____
2. _____   7. _____
3. _____   8. _____
4. _____   9. _____
5. _____ 10. _____

Chapter 7 Memory Techniques

Exercise 3

Your instructor is going to divide you into groups, each of which will create two abbreviations representing something you have learned in this class. At the end of the time limit, you will share your abbreviations with the rest of the class.

OUR ABBREVIATIONS:

THE CLASS'S ABBREVIATIONS:

Chapter 7   Memory Techniques

Exercise 4

1. Take five minutes to draw a cluster representing what you know about memory techniques.

   At the end of the five minutes, your instructor will ask you to join in a discussion about this memory method.

Chapter 7   Memory Techniques

Exercise 5

It's the Fabulous Memory Game Show!

Your instructor is going to divide you into teams. Each team will receive two minutes to look at a tray filled with several small items. At the end of the two minutes, your instructor will ask a series of questions that you will answer below. The team or teams with the best memories will get a fabulous prize.

1. _____
2. _____
3. _____
4. _____
5. _____
6. _____
7. _____
8. _____
9. _____
10. _____

Case Study

Forgetful Patty

Patty O'Brien has just started school as a Business major. During the first week of her Introduction to Computer class, she is assigned a list of terms for a quiz. Watching TV, she picks up the list consisting of the following terms: software, hardware, diskette, terminal, laser printer, CRT, dot matrix printer, internal hard drive, modem, mouse, and laptop. After studying these terms for ten minutes, she watches her favorite half-hour program and then tries to write down the list of twelve terms. But all she can remember are software and diskette. Frustrated, she dumps the books by the front door and assures her mother that she'll study tomorrow in the breakroom before class.

1. What techniques could Patty use to help her remember the twelve terms?

2. What changes does Patty need to make in her study habits if she hopes to be successful?

3. If you were Patty's best friend, what would you tell her about the effort it takes to reach one's goals?

Suggested Resource Material

Books: Additional Resources

Lorayne, Harry. *How to Develop Super Power Memory.* NAL-Dutton Publishing Co., 1974.

Brown, Alan S., Ph.D. *How to Increase Your Memory Power.* Scott, Foresman Professional Books Publishing Co., 1989.

Lorayne, Harry, & Lucas, Jerry. *The Memory Book.* Ballantine Publishing Co., 1986.

Chapter 8

Test-Taking Techniques

"I know that learning and earning go hand in hand, and I enjoy both."

Personal Comment Sheet

Entry Date

Five self-positives:

1.

2.

3.

4.

5.

Getting Focused

How do I think the information I am about to read will help me reach my goals?

Anxiety and fear seem to be the natural partners of tests. Why? Most people believe that tests are cruel and unjust punishment because in their minds so much depends on the test score. If you receive an "A," does that automatically mean that you are an "A" person? On the other hand if you receive an "F," does that make you an "F" person? If this concept were true, the majority of successful people would not be successful. A test score is not a total reflection of your ability to contribute to society; it is simply a measure of how well you interpreted information on one given test on one given day. The result of a test depends on knowing the information, but it also depends on the amount of anxiety and nervousness a person experiences during the test.

Prepare Mentally for Test Taking

Athletes, actors, and astronauts, just to mention a few, feel the same anxiety and nervousness before their events, but they are taught to psych themselves up before a big game, a performance, or a launch. By practicing positive self-talk, and using their nervous energy to focus their concentration on reaching their goals, they turn anxiety into excellence.

Figure 8-1

Actors learn to prepare mentally for their performances

Photo by Richard Younker

How can you psych yourself up? First, believe in yourself and your ability. Visualize specific situations you have experienced in the past where you felt nervous but overcame that feeling to accomplish the task successfully. Remind yourself of all the great conditioning you have done to prepare yourself to be successful. Restate your belief that this test simply measures what you know at a point in time, and that you look forward to the guidance it will give you by either signaling that you are indeed ready to go on or need to go back and review. Always end this psych session by reconfirming your confidence in your ability to succeed through hard work and self-reliance. Take time now to write out your personal psych statements.

Relieve Test Anxiety

Marla sits in the back of her Introduction to Electronics class and waits for the instructor to hand out the test forms. With her heart pounding in her ears, she rubs her clammy hands in an attempt to dry them on her jeans. As the instructor gets closer, she feels cold chills run down her back and mentally relives every test she has done poorly on.

It's not hard to imagine how miserable Marla's behavior makes her feel. However, right off we can spot an area that she could work on. She isn't psyching herself up, is she? Instead, she is choosing to remember every awful test experience she has ever had. This type of behavior only adds to her anxiety. Once she learns to psych herself up, what else can she do?

Practice Deep Breathing By learning and practicing some simple deep breathing exercises, Marla can learn to relax. What types of exercises can you do? Start by sitting up straight at your desk with your feet flat on the floor. Now close your eyes and clear your mind of everything but the tension you are feeling in your body. Inhale slowly and hold it for a second. Start with your feet; as you exhale slowly, feel yourself letting the tension flow out of your feet. Move up to your ankles and repeat the procedure. Do this with each limb of your body right up to your head, letting the tension flow out each time you exhale. When you open your eyes, tell yourself you are relaxed, confident, and ready to go. Practice this technique until you feel comfortable with it.

Be Aware of Surroundings Another way to relax is to be aware of your surroundings. Chances are the room used for the test is the same room you have sat in every day prior to the test. It is not a chamber equipped with mirrors to show everyone how nervous you are.

Have Appropriate Supplies As a professional test taker, you need to come to each test prepared. In the area of supplies you should have at the minimum a pen or pencil, paper (if it is not provided), and a watch so that you can keep track of the time. For those of you who wear glasses, make sure they are clean and smudge-free. If, like Marla, you suffer from "clammy hands syndrome," it's a good idea to have a handkerchief. What other types of supplies can you think of that a professional test taker could use?

Remove Any Mental Clutter Just like Marla, many of us before a test allow our minds to fill with clutter. In her case she relived every bad test experience. Your mind clutter may include thoughts about how much smarter everyone is than you, self-doubts about how much study time you put in, or old messages about what a failure you are. Can you see how this type of mental clutter keeps you from doing your best?

How can you counteract it? Remember, you can control the thoughts that enter your mind. Block this mind clutter by filling your brain with more positive statements. Remind yourself of how much time you have spent reading and studying this information.

Keep in mind that it's only a test — a reflection of what you know, not of who you are or what you're worth. Mentally repeat your psych statements until you see this clutter float away.

Be On Time Being on time for class will give your mind time to prepare to sort through the information you will need. Rushing into the room just as the test is being handed out does not give you time to mentally or physically prepare to be successful. That is why professional baseball and football players arrive at the stadium hours before the game.

If you arrive five minutes early, is this a good time to do a little last minute cramming? No, because it will only serve to confuse you. Your mind needs time and repeated exposure to information before it can accurately retain and retrieve it. If you have not studied, right before the test is not the time to panic. But it is the time to make a promise to yourself to change your study habits.

Study for the Test

If you saw yourself in the last paragraph and are ready to change or just want to do better on the test, how should you go about it?

Review Material Daily Schedule review time daily to go over the information you have received that day. Make clear notes and remember that if you read it, say it, and then write it, you are using three of your senses to lock in the information. At the end of the week you should review all the material you have received. Take into consideration that this is something you must do every day and every week. The brain needs time to absorb information, especially complicated subjects, and that is why cramming for a test will not help you to retain the information. The more times you put the information into your brain the more you lock it in, so you will be able to access it later.

If you are reviewing for an open-book test, take a separate piece of paper and write down any formulas or key definitions you will need. Use paper clips or staple notes to index pages so you don't waste time looking for pages you know in advance will be important. And most of all, don't make the common mistake of assuming that because the test is open-book it will be easier.

Use Outlines As you study and review, write out the headings and key ideas from your chapters. This activity allows you to summarize the most important information. Remember to leave a wide one-and- a-half- to two-inch margin so that you can write any questions you have about the information directly on your outline. Then by going back to the textbook, material listed in the bibliography, or your instructor, you can find the answers to these questions.

This step is particularly important if you have an open-book test. With an open-book test, it is a good idea to organize your notes and outlines by numbering them. Then make a short table of contents so that you can quickly find the information you need during the test.

Anticipate Questions By anticipating test questions during your review time, you can improve your test scores. To do this, role play the instructor and give yourself questions that you think might be on the test. Study groups are ideal for this type of activity. Where do these possible test questions come from? A good place to start is with the key headings in your book. One question you could expect from this chapter is "What are five things you can do to relieve test anxiety?" Another place to look for question ideas is in your notes and any end of chapter questions.

Summarize Material Write down what you have learned in your own words without the benefit of notes or textbooks. By summarizing what you know, you will be able to spot areas that you are hazy on. Then compare these notes with your textbook and class notes to fill in vague areas of information you have missed completely.

Observe Some General Guidelines for Taking Tests

Runji Komuro has practiced his deep breathing skills, cleared his mind of mental clutter, and reviewed the material daily. Since he's taken this kind of test at least a zillion times, when the instructor hands him the test he starts right in answering question number one. Unfortunately, Runji has already made two mistakes. Can you spot them?

Follow Directions By assuming that he knew how to take this type of test, Runji made his first mistake. Nothing is more frustrating than doing poorly on a test because you did not take the time to read the instructions. Be sure that you don't make this mistake by reading and then rereading the directions. Get them clear in your mind before you even glance at the first question. What was Runji's second mistake? He failed to follow the advice in the next section.

Scan the Test Do a quick scan of the entire test, paying close attention to the value of each section. By doing a quick check of the test and the point value of each section, you will be able to judge how much time you will need to schedule for each section. You do not want to spend twenty minutes out of fifty minutes on a section of the test worth only ten points out of a hundred.

Know When to Ask Questions Know what the rules are for asking the instructor questions during the test, and what materials are allowed in the room.

Develop a Test-Taking Strategy

When a football team steps out onto the playing field, they have a game plan to help them win. To do your best on a test, you also need a game plan.

Figure 8-2

Developing a test-taking strategy helps to relieve test anxiety.

George Bellerose/Stock, Boston

Answer Easy Questions First

By answering the easy questions first, you accomplish two things. This strategy allows you to experience success and stimulates associations that prepare your mind for more difficult questions.

Usually the easiest questions are fill-in-the-blank and true-false. After you answer these, go to the multiple-choice and short-answer questions. This strategy allows you to save the essay questions, which are usually the most difficult and time consuming, for last.

Practice Time Management

Watch the time and pace yourself; if you are stuck, move on to a question you can answer. Follow your time plan and don't get distracted.

Use Space Wisely

Write small enough so that you leave plenty of blank space between your answers. This space makes it easier for you to go back and add additional information to your answer; also it is easier for the instructor to grade your work if it is not all crammed together.

Get Clues from Other Questions

If you are stuck on a question, look at the other questions on the test and your answers. The other questions may jog your memory, or you may even find the information you need (a date, name, etc.) in one of the other questions.

Follow Your First Instinct

In multiple-choice or true-false questions your first instinct is usually correct. It's always good advice not to change your answer unless you are very sure the second choice is right. Of course, do change your answer if you are wrong because you didn't read the question correctly.

How to Handle Specific Question Types

Now that you have a general game plan, it's time to get down to specifics. Knowing how best to handle each type of question helps relieve test anxiety and raises your scores.

True-False Questions

Always answer true-false questions quickly. In most instances individual true-false questions are not worth a lot of points, so don't spend a great deal of time struggling over 1 point on a 100-point exam.

Remember, a statement is false if any part of it is false. When you read the question, look for words like "sometimes," "all," "most," or "never." These words are known as qualifiers and the question depends on them. Sentences that contain "always" or "never" are almost always false. For example, one of your test questions states, "Successful students always remember facts by putting them to music." The word "always" makes this statement false. Using this example, replace the word "always" with "never." The statement is still false, isn't it? What if you replace "always" with "sometimes"?

Multiple-Choice Questions

Ana Cruz completes the true-false questions quickly and then reads the instructions for the multiple-choice section carefully. The first question is "How often should you review study material?" Before looking at the choices, she answers in her head. Next she reads the possible answers: A. Once a month, B. Before a test, C. At the end of every week, and D. All of the above. Finding that D matches the answer she came up with, she marks it and proceeds to the next question. Unable to remember the answer to this one, she puts a check mark to the left of it so she can come back to it later. Watching Ana take this section of the test, it is obvious that she has the skills of a professional test taker. What tipped us off?

First, she took time to read the directions for this section. Some tests may instruct you to choose only the best answer while others may have one or more correct answers for every question. Like Ana, before you do anything else, make sure you understand the instructions.

Can you spot the next smart move Ana made? When looking at the first question she answered it in her head before she looked at her choices. By doing this, she came up with the correct answer so she would not get confused by the wording in the choices. Also, she was not surprised or thrown off by the fact that one of her choices was "all of the above." She knew that test questions could contain this expression or "none of the above," or "both A and B." Taking this possibility into consideration, she did not make the mistake of just cramming for one good answer for every question.

What did she do when she couldn't answer the next question? Rather than wasting valuable time trying to remember the answer, she simply put a check mark next to the question. By doing this, if something on the test triggers her memory, she can find the question quickly. If she has time at the end of the test her check marks will make it easy for her to see which questions she still needs to work on. What if she goes back to the questions and still can't think of the answer? Since unanswered questions will also be counted wrong, she has nothing to lose by making an educated guess.

How can you turn a wild guess into an educated guess? When a question is written so that your answer completes the sentence, to make an educated guess, throw out any answers that do not form a grammatically correct sentence. If you are required to choose from a wide range of numbers (8.2, 44.5, 66.8, 700.12) your best bet is to choose one in the middle. What if instead of numbers you have to choose from three answers, two of which are worded similarly? Again, if an unmarked answer will also be counted wrong, choose the most likely of these two answers. This advice also applies to questions for which the answers are measurements or amounts. If two are similar, choose one of them. While these suggestions will help you guess, don't depend on them to pass a test. If you have taken the time to correctly learn the information, your educated guessing skills should be used infrequently.

Short-Answer/Fill-in-the-Blank Questions

These types of questions usually require definitions of terms or short descriptions. An example of a fill-in-the-blank question would be, "When you are answering true-false questions you should circle your answers _____." As you read this question if you filled in the blank with the word "quickly," you are absolutely right. Keep your answers brief and work quickly through these sections by looking for facts or key words.

When you have studied effectively, the answers to these questions should come to you easily. Use grammar to help you decide on the answer; for instance, if the word "an" appears before a blank you know the answer begins with a vowel, and if "a" appears before the blank the answer begins with a consonant. However, don't depend on these types of clues to help you pass the test. If the test has been prepared by a textbook company, it is almost guaranteed that these types of hints have been eliminated long before it hits your desk.

Essay Questions

Even for the best test takers, essay questions can make their mouths go dry and hands get clammy. They scare us because they are a true test of our knowledge. With no choices, blanks, or sentences to use as a guide, nothing can expose us quicker than an essay question and lots of blank space waiting to be filled. How can you take the fear out of these questions?

Before you start to answer an essay question, make sure you understand exactly what the question is asking. Then make a quick outline of the main points you want to cover in your answer. Although usually you will answer these questions last, it is a good idea to write this brief outline at the start of the test period. This allows you to add other ideas or facts that come to you as you answer the other questions on the test. When you are ready to begin writing your answer, this outline will allow you to write faster and help insure that you don't leave out necessary facts. And if you run out of time before completing the answer, the outline may gain you some points.

When you are ready to start writing, it is a good idea to start with a brief introductory sentence. For example, if one of your essay questions was, "Explain the three different types of goals," a good introductory sentence would be, "When setting goals you will develop long-term, intermediate, and short-term goals." This sentence jumps right into your answer and shows that you know some key terms related to goal setting. After this introductory sentence, you would go on to explain in more detail the purpose of each type of goal and how they work together to help you reach the objectives you have set. As you formulate your answer in your mind, using your outline as a guide, remember to include the key ideas first. Then if you have time you can go into more detail. After you complete your answer, check the following things to boost your chances of a good score. Is your handwriting clear and easy for the instructor to read? Did you cut out any filler sentences that just take up space? Is your answer grammatically correct and has all spelling been double-checked? Did you write the answer as if the person reading it had little if any knowledge about the subject matter?

With the above information in mind, let's peek over the shoulders of two students, Alice and Kathy, whose names were changed to protect their identities. Both are given the essay question "Explain deep breathing exercises and how they can help relieve test anxiety."

Alice gets her test, reads the basic instructions, and then flips back to the essay question. On the left-hand margin she quickly writes a rough outline of the following key ideas: close eyes, clear mind, inhale slowly and hold, exhale feeling tension flow first from feet and then work way up body, relieving tension from body allows mind to concentrate on test. After answering the rest of the test questions, she returns to the essay question and begins formulating an answer in her mind. Knowing that an introductory sentence is important, she begins her answer with "The purpose of deep breathing exercises is to allow the body to release tension before a test so that the mind can concentrate free of interference." She follows her opening sentence with the rest of her answer: "The first step in deep breathing exercises is to close your eyes and clear your mind. After inhaling slowly and holding your breath, exhale while picturing the tension leaving your feet. Continue inhaling, holding this breath, and then exhaling as you visualize each part of your body relaxing, all the way to the top of your head."

Now let's check in and see how Kathy is doing. Opening the test, she goes right to the first section, which is multiple-choice, and answers them in order. With several questions, she has trouble deciding which answer to choose but, determined to do well, she concentrates on each until the answer comes to her. Finally finishing this section, she goes on to the short-answer questions. After spending ten minutes with one short-answer question worth five points, she smiles as she goes to the next section. So far she feels good about her performance on the test. Again, she takes her time on the fill-in-the-blank section. Quickly marking the true-false questions, she turns to the essay question just as the instructor announces that there are only two minutes left. Trying to beat the clock she begins to write: "Deep breathing exercises are important because they help you on a test. You feel better when you have done some deep breathing exercises and this will show in your scores. You should start these exercises before

Figure 8-3

You be the judge. Score 2 points for each Test-Taking Strategy used. Highest score is the winner.

Scorecard for Kathy
10 points possible

STRATEGY	POINTS
Read Directions	_____
Scanned Test	_____
Answered Essay Questions first	_____
Practiced Time Management	_____
Outlined Essay Questions	_____
Total Points	_____
Essay Grade	_____

Scorecard for Alice
10 points possible

STRATEGY	POINTS
Read Directions	_____
Scanned Test	_____
Answered Essay Questions first	_____
Practiced Time Management	_____
Outlined Essay Questions	_____
Total Points	_____
Essay Grade	_____

Creating Your Own Success

the test is handed out so that you don't waste time. To begin a deep breathing exercise you need to close your . . . " At this point the instructor calls for all exams to be brought to the front of the room. Kathy does not even have time to finish her last sentence; while Alice has used the last five minutes to go back and decide on answers to the questions she left check marks next to. Both feeling good about their performances, they leave our example and go to the mall for some major window shopping. While they are out having fun, you get a chance to be their instructor. What test strategies did they use effectively when taking this exam? What mistakes, if any, did they make? Grade both of their essay answers using the guidelines we have discussed and be prepared to explain your reasons for the grades you give.

Who Gets Cheated?

You walk into a fine restaurant and are seated at a table next to an attractive couple who proceed to pay for their dinners in advance. Since this is a little odd, you find yourself watching them out of the corner of your eye. When their meals are served, the man pokes at his plate but does not eat anything, even though he comments that the food is fine and just what he asked for. The woman takes a bite of her food, holds it in her mouth, and then spits it back on the plate. After the couple leaves, you ask the waiter about them and he comments that this is not unusual, that they do it all the time. Naturally you can't imagine why someone would choose to pay for something and then refuse to take advantage of it. But this is exactly what you do if you cheat or cram for a test. The man in the restaurant did not hurt the owner; the restaurant still got paid; the chef still got a salary; the only person who lost out was the customer. The same applies to you if you cheat. The school still gets your tuition, your instructor still receives a salary, but you, through your own choice, have paid for knowledge that you have not gotten. Cheating may seem smart at the time, and you may even fool one or two instructors, but you won't fool an employer once it's found out you can't do the work for which you were hired. You won't feel very clever unemployed and in debt for an education you refused to take advantage of.

Now let's talk about Miss Spit-It-Out. She is getting a little more benefit for her money by at least tasting the food, but is not fooling her body into thinking she's given it anything to operate on. This is just like cramming. When you put information in your mind without giving it time to thoroughly "digest" it, the information is stored only in short-term memory. You may be able to "spit out" some of it for the test, but you are getting no long-term benefit from the very information that you came to school to learn. Though you may have access to it for the test, when the real test of employment comes around this information will be no more than a distant recollection. Employers aren't interested in paying for knowledge you knew for two days six months ago. Next time you think about cheating or cramming, just remember who you're hurting.

Chapter 8

More Steps On My Road To Success
A Personal Review

1. What were the key concepts discussed about test taking?

2. How do I plan to put this new test-taking knowledge into effect?

3. What are the areas I don't understand or need more information on?

4. What is my game plan for getting the additional information I need?

5. What positive changes do I see in myself?

Chapter 8   Test-Taking Techniques

Exercise 1

The purpose of this exercise is to help you formulate a plan of action to combat test anxiety. Use the test-taking techniques discussed in class to formulate a step-by-step plan of action. Be positive and forceful in designing your plan of action. Start each step with a positive statement that clearly says you are in command.

Suggested steps you might use are:

Step 1.   List everything you will do to prepare for the test.

Step 2.   List all of the reasons you can think of for testing — for example, "Tests provide me with valuable feedback on my progress. I need this feedback before proceeding to the next phase of a subject."

Step 3. List all of the steps you will take from the time you sit down in the exam room until the time you actually start the test.

Step 4. List all of the steps you will take during the test

Step 5. Write a short paragraph to help psych yourself up before a test.

Chapter 8 Test-Taking Techniques

Exercise 2

Using any of the types of questions — essay, multiple choice, true-false, or fill-in-the-blank — write down two sample test questions and their answers for each of the chapters you have covered in this book. Remember to pick material that will help review the main points you have learned so far. Once you have completed your questions, turn them in to your instructor.

Chapter 8 Test-Taking Techniques

Exercise 3

Knowledge of the following words is essential to giving the right answers on a test. In the space provided, write out a brief definition of what each word is asking you to do, then check the dictionary to see if you are right.

1. Cite _____
2. Define _____
3. Enumerate _____
4. Give _____
5. Identify _____
6. Interpret _____
7. Indicate _____
8. List _____
9. Mention _____
10. Name _____
11. Prove _____
12. State _____
13. Compare _____
14. Contrast _____
15. Describe _____
16. Develop _____
17. Diagram _____
18. Discuss _____
19. Illustrate _____
20. Outline _____
21. Review _____

22. Sketch _____

23. Summarize _____

24. Trace _____

25. In what types of questions are you most likely to find these words?

    _____

    _____

26. By looking up the meaning of the words you were not familiar with, you have just strengthened your vocabulary. In what ways could a large vocabulary help someone reach their goals?

    _____

    _____

    _____

    _____

    _____

Case Study

Deron Looks at His Future

Deron left high school when he was 17 because of problems at home and in school. After spending three years in various shelters, he realized he was living the only future he would ever have unless he got some skills. Trying to turn his life around, he moved back home and enrolled in college. His academic adviser had him start with some basic classes to help him reach the skill levels of the other students. Deron uses his time wisely when he is in school, but finds himself drawn back to the streets when classes let out. His best friend from the last shelter, Louie, makes fun of him, calling Deron's remedial textbooks "baby books" and reminding him that none of their friends has even a full-time job, let alone the corporate one that Deron dreams of. Shrugging off Louie's comments, he goes to school, but the sound of his best friend laughing at him rings in his ears. Deron tries to ignore his self-doubts, but as he opens his reading textbook he feels humiliated as he struggles with the simple words. Just as he slams the book shut, Mr. Braun begins passing out a test that Deron has completely forgotten about. Deron feels his heart begin to beat fast, and the idea that he will follow Louie's advice and quit if he fails this test begins to whirl through his mind. Opening up the test form, he stares at the first question for ten minutes, his mind blank.

1. Taking into consideration all the things you have learned in class so far, what are some of the main issues Deron needs to address if he is to be successful?

2. If you could rewrite this story, what would you have Deron say to Louie when he makes fun of his books and his goals?

3. What could Deron have thought when he got the test that would have given him a better chance for long-term success?

Suggested Resource Material

Books: Additional Resources

Walker, C. E. *Learn to Relax—13 Ways to Reduce Tension.* Prentice-Hall Publishing Inc., 1975.

Chapter 9
Body Language and Appearance

"I use every opportunity to make a good impression."

Personal Comment Sheet

Entry Date _____

Five self-positives:

1. _____

2. _____

3. _____

4. _____

5. _____

Getting Focused

How do I think the information I am about to read will help me reach my goals?

_____
_____
_____
_____
_____
_____

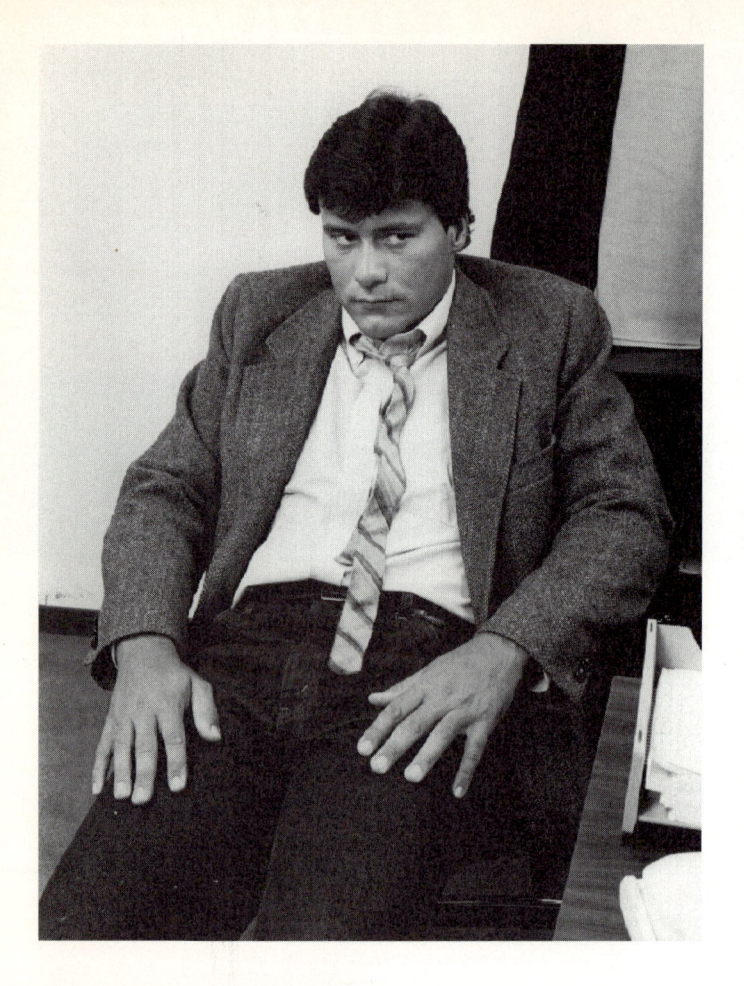

Figure 9-1

Would you hire this person?

Your boss rushes into your office and explains a last-minute change in plans. Two work-study students have been sent to spend the day and she needs you to take charge of one of them. Allowing you first choice, she gives you thirty seconds to decide. By glancing around the corner of your office, you can see both students. One is slouched against the file cabinets, his jacket dumped on the floor at his feet. He wears torn jeans, a baggy sweatshirt, orange high-top tennis shoes, and is chewing gum. While carelessly stuffing the office newsletter he was given in his back jeans pocket, he tries to flirt with your assistant. The other student has dressed in pressed navy slacks, a white dress shirt, and navy patterned tie. He is standing up straight and reading the newsletter. Seeing you, he smiles and then returns his attention to his reading. Which student would you choose to spend eight hours with?

Since you did not get a chance to speak to either student, you had to make your decision based on two visual signals — body language and appearance. Often, these two visual signals form the basis for our first impressions. We see someone, notice their appearance, judge their body language, and then decide what we think about them. We do this so quickly that most times we aren't even aware of what has happened. Instantly our brains process these visual signals and we say in the simplest terms, I like this person or I don't, I feel comfortable with this person or I don't. Accepting that we too are judged this way allows us to tailor our body language and appearance to our advantage.

Body Language

In the Listening chapter (Chapter 3) you learned that good eye contact is an important part of communicating. But what is body language? It is any nonverbal message we send through our facial expressions and body movements. People study body language in hopes of clearer communication. Though it is not a science, being aware of body language, both yours and others, is important. Learning how to successfully communicate through the appropriate use of nonverbal communication is a powerful tool to help you reach your goals.

Body Language, the Nonverbal Communication

We learn the languages we speak by listening to those around us. We learn to use body language in much the same way. If our cultural background is Spanish-American we may have been exposed to a different body language than a child raised in a Japanese-American family. A person who grew up in the South may use a gesture that in the North is totally misunderstood. One day the fact that you are rubbing your forehead may be a sign that you are extremely irritated, while another day it may just mean that you have a headache.

The most obvious messages we communicate using body language are anger, fear, love, happiness, sadness, and power. Before going on, it should be pointed out that people also learn to hide their emotions by using body language. Choosing a more appropriate body language than we might feel at the moment and self-discipline go hand in hand. Without the ability to mask emotions, people would be in constant conflict.

Types of Messages

We send out body language messages both consciously and subconsciously. The messages we send out subconsciously are called conditioned-reflex body language. When you jump at an unexpected noise, or your eyes widen at a surprise, you are displaying conditioned-reflex body language. This type of body language is usually difficult to change. But it can be done. By repeatedly exposing ourselves to loud noises, we could train ourselves to ignore them completely. But what about the other type of body language, the kind we are supposed to send consciously?

Bud Grimson has never taken the time to think about his body language. He prides himself on being open and honest. You might say he wears his emotions on his sleeve. If somebody makes him mad, they know it before he even says a word. The minute he feels anger, without even thinking, he sends out the following signals: stands rigid, jaw jutted out, fists jammed into his pants pockets, eyes cold and unblinking. How effective will this type of body language be with his boss? His employees? His family? Because he has never been conscious of his body language, for every emotion he has only one set of responses. By not learning to choose from a variety of appropriate body language, he is hurting his chance for success.

How have we learned to show other emotions? Fear is often displayed by clutching our bodies as if to protect ourselves from whatever has frightened us. We may open our eyes very wide or even faint. As the body releases adrenaline, some people even acquire superhuman strength.

Love communication has a wide range of body messages — for example, flirting. This message can be communicated with a glance, wink, smile, and of course with suggestive body movements. There are many species of animals that indulge in ritual body movements to entice their mates. Parents display tenderness and compassion for their young, but they can also represent authority with a look or a stance and folded arms. There are many forms of love — parents', children's, romantic, siblings', friendship — and each of these has its own set of body messages.

Defending our space is yet another form of body language. One example of this is people on an elevator. The next time you are on an elevator, be aware of how everyone, including yourself, tries not to touch the people next to them. People on an elevator will look straight ahead, each sending out the message that this is "my space." Huge crowds can become very nervous over the lack of individual space. Notice where you sit in a lecture hall or in the classroom. Do you sit at the back of the room, trying to secure a certain amount of anonymity, even though you can't hear or see as well? Or do you sit up front where you can hear and see comfortably, but where you will be noticed?

Many people use body language to give the impression of power and authority. People who display authority seem to take up a lot of space. They stand with feet slightly apart and elbows bent, both of which create the image of a dominant figure. How we use space or guard space tells others how we see ourselves, as dominant or subservient.

To help you become more aware, watch the body language of people driving cars, standing in lines, and sitting in restaurants. Notice what kind of body messages the people around you are sending out. You have been sending out body messages without thinking all your life — now try doing it consciously. By being aware of what kind of messages we are sending, we can become more effective communicators.

Matching the Movement to the Message

How do you learn to make your body movements reinforce the message you are trying to relay? Practice, practice. It's great advice to practice, but what if you have no idea where to begin? In several places throughout this book you have been encouraged to turn off the TV. Well, now we want you to turn it on, but not just for entertainment. If one group of people understand the power of body language, it is professional actors and actresses. As they prepare for a role, they practice over and over making the gesture appropriate for the words. Choose several different types of programs on TV and study how the characters use their bodies to punch up a laugh or capture an emotion. Can you spot times when the words and actions don't go together? This technique is often used by comics to get a laugh. And now back to practice. Taking what you have learned, as you choose your words, make a conscious choice to also use body language that will give your words added power.

As you work on making your movements match your message, pay particular attention to any nervous gestures you might have. Since you are going to be conscious of your body language, now is a great time to rid yourself of "detractors" like cracking your knuckles, playing with your jewelry, or pushing your glasses up on your nose. Why do you think we call these bad habits "detractors"? Can you think of any other nervous gestures people should check for?

Appearance

Let's look back at our opening example of the two work-study students. With only thirty seconds to make your decision, you based part of it on their body language. But the other part was based on appearance. By choosing the navy slacks, white shirt, and navy patterned tie, the one work-study student communicated through his appearance that he understood the professionalism required to be successful. The other student's choice of clothes gave an entirely different message.

It may not seem fair, but people will judge you by your appearance. You can rebel against this and, using only your own likes and dislikes as a guide, develop a wardrobe and appearance that is totally unique. But do not be surprised if you suffer some consequences from your choices. Or you can take the other approach and use this time in school to polish your appearance so that it reflects the standards of your chosen profession.

Nearly every occupation has its own image. In certain occupations and professions the image tends to reinforce the credibility of the occupation. For instance, we expect to see a doctor in his/her office or hospital dressed in a white clinical jacket. We would feel very uncomfortable and doubtful of the doctor's ability if he/she was dressed in cutoff shorts and sandals. The same thing holds true for football players. Imagine your reaction if the quarterback for the Dallas Cowboys came out on the field dressed in tights, ballet slippers, and a tutu. Not what you would expect, right?

To reinforce this theory, make a list of professions and the type of images you expect to see in those professions.

Examples:
Lawyers	Bankers	Computer programmers
Judges	Secretaries	Fashion buyers
Medical assistants	Automobile sales people	Accountants

One Chance to Make a Good First Impression

A student was once overheard making the remark that "Appearances are just a game." The instructor's response was "Yes, it is a game, the game of being able to tell the person who wants to be a professional from one who doesn't." You only have one chance to make a good first impression, and most first impressions are

Figure 9-2

Much of what people think about you stems from the way you look.

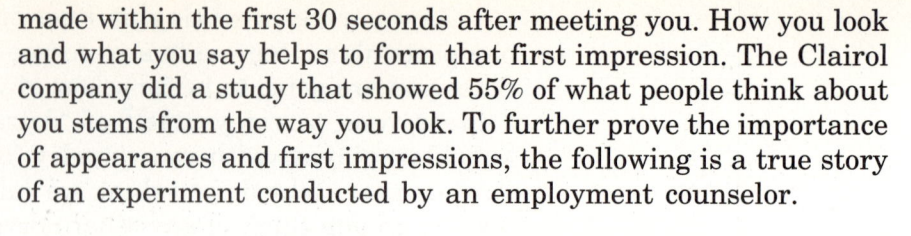

made within the first 30 seconds after meeting you. How you look and what you say helps to form that first impression. The Clairol company did a study that showed 55% of what people think about you stems from the way you look. To further prove the importance of appearances and first impressions, the following is a true story of an experiment conducted by an employment counselor.

The Experiment

The story begins with a job opening for an administrative assistant in a local company. The personnel director of this company happened to be a friend of the person staging this experiment; however, the personnel director was not told about the experiment until after the fact. The personnel director was contacted and asked if she would be interested in interviewing two prospective graduates for the position available in her company. She was indeed interested in interviewing the two people and so the experiment began. The interviews were scheduled for Judy and Jill; both Judy and Jill were the same person.

Judy's interview was scheduled first. She arrived on time, dressed in very casual attire. Her hair was clean, but not styled. It was difficult to see her face. She wore no makeup and chose a very large purse as an accessory. She wore sunglasses throughout the interview, and emphasized her accent so her voice would not be recognized. Judy's resumé was perfect and she answered the questions professionally.

The second interview was scheduled with Jill. She also arrived on time. For this interview she had chosen a very flattering business suit. She chose her accessories very carefully right down to her conservative coordinated shoes. Her hair was styled and she wore the appropriate amount of makeup. Jill's resumé was different than Judy's, but it was just as perfect. She interviewed in the same professional manner as Judy. Incidentally, our interviewee's real name is Jill. Jill related how the two interviews had gone. Judy's interview had not lasted as long as Jill's, with not as many questions asked. She had taken the same employment tests both times, and answered the interviewer's questions much the same both times. Jill was asked to return for a second interview; Judy was not. Jill was given a tour of the facility; Judy was not.

A few days after Jill's interview, the personnel director called the employment counselor and thanked her for sending the two very qualified applicants. The interviewer related that both of the ladies had scored the same on their employment tests; however, they were very impressed with Jill. She had the exact qualifications and professional appearance they were looking for. Keep in mind that both of their qualifications were the same. The personnel director scheduled a second interview with Jill, where intentions were to hire her. Jill had her second interview — or was this really the third interview? She accepted the position and started her new career a week later.

When the personnel director was finally told about the experiment, she at first did not believe that Judy and Jill were the same person. It was explained to her in detail the reason for the experiment and she agreed it was a success. She also agreed to document the story so it could be told to future prospective graduates. The moral of the story: Good skills are absolutely necessary, but a professional appearance and good first impression are the clinchers.

A Well-Packaged Product

Leaving school after class, you drop by the grocery store to pick up something for dinner. Hungry for chicken soup, you find everyone else must have had the same craving because only two cans are left. One has a professionally designed label carefully wrapped and sealed around the can. The label clearly shows the contents and gives nutritional information. Examining the other brand, you notice that the label was cut too small to fit around the can, leaving a great deal of metal exposed. The next thing that catches your eye is the fact that the label was put on crooked and big globs of dried glue are sticking out along all of the edges. Trying to read the nutritional information, you find the print so small it is impossible to read. You decide that a company willing to produce such a sloppy-looking product probably isn't too particular about how the soup tastes either, and put it back on the shelf. Having chosen the more professional-looking product, you head for the checkout stand. Have you made your decision fairly?

There are those who would say you haven't. They would argue that only the contents of the package should be judged. But others would say that your decision was a fair one. In today's fast-paced society, we often use outward appearances to judge the product. This is why most companies take the appearance of their employees seriously.

When a company hires you, you become part of their professional image. They realize that if your appearance is sloppy or unprofessional, their customers may question if this lack of attention to detail carries over into your work. They also know that customers may also read your appearance as a sign that the company lacks pride; otherwise the company would step in and require you to correct your appearance. Can you think of a time when a person's appearance caused you not to want to do business with the company they represented?

Why should you worry about becoming a well-packaged product now? By developing a more professional appearance while you are in school, you will be helping to boost your self-confidence. Just like any of the other skills in this book, it takes practice to develop your own professional style. School is a great place to try out a variety of looks without damaging your career. In addition, polishing your appearance now will make a favorable impression on your instructors, administrators, guest speakers, and possible future employers that may tour your school.

All of this sounds great, but where do you begin? Let's start at the top. The hairstyle you choose makes a very personal statement. Is it wild and uncontrolled? Is it pulled back in a tight knot? Have you shaved your head completely? Or let it grow long below your shoulders? Each of these styles might be appropriate for a different business. A professional model might do well with the first one, while an Olympic swimmer might choose to shave his head to help him increase his speed. Although this is a personal choice, there are some basic guidelines. Avoid choosing a style that covers your eyes, because this interferes with your ability to communicate effectively. Remember how often we have mentioned the importance of good eye contact? If you color your hair, do touch-ups at least once a month so the roots do not show. Men with long hair or beards should be aware that these choices do not fit the image of many companies. When you are choosing a new hairstyle, look through fashion magazines, catalogs, and at the people you see in your local businesses. Then, use the advice of a professional salon to help guide you. Don't be afraid to tell a stylist that you are working toward a more professional image. They can be good sources of information about what is professionally fashionable in your community.

Now that your hair looks great, let's move to your hands. This is an area where fashion moves quickly. One season long bright nails are in and by summer they are to be kept short and pale. The best advice is to wear them short. Employers tend to wonder how much work you'll accomplish with long dragon nails. If you polish your nails, choose colors that compliment your skin, while avoiding those that are too iridescent or dark. When polish becomes chipped, remove it. If you're a guy, surely you don't have to worry about your hands, do you? Wrong. You just have to concern yourself with fewer choices. Keep your nails clean, neatly trimmed, and watch those cuticles. If the back edges of your nails look like a shark has been chewing on them, buy a cuticle-removing cream, follow the directions, and then use it regularly. Since most of us use our hands to gesture and add emphasis to our words, their professional upkeep is very important.

While you are at the local salon getting your hair and nails done, Mrs. Therdor bursts through the door. Though she is a size fourteen, she refuses to admit it and continually tries to squeeze into size tens. This morning's effort to do so has left her slightly breathless and bulging everywhere. Walking past where you are sitting, she leaves a suffocating trail of perfume that is doing a poor job of covering the fact that she has not bathed. Digging in her purse, she gets out her makeup bag and starts slathering on another layer of eye shadow, lipstick, and blush. Having nothing better to do while your nails dry, you begin to count the appearance mistakes Mrs. Therdor has made.

One of the first rules of choosing clothes is to pick the right size for you. Not all of us are a size two or even want to be. Your clothes should be neither too large nor too tight. By refusing to admit the truth about her size, Mrs Therdor is fooling no one but herself. This is also true with trying to cover poor personal hygiene by bathing in cologne. Perfume or aftershave should be worn lightly. If applied with a heavy hand it not only smells too strong but can cause allergic reactions in other people. You want to take people's breath away because of your professional appearance, not because they can't stand to inhale when they are around you. At the very minimum you should use soap, water, and deodorant on a daily basis. How about Mrs. Therdor's use of makeup? We can guess from the description that she likes to apply it pretty thick. Makeup should be worn to accentuate your features, not to drown them out. The difference between good and bad makeup application is the difference between candlelight and neon. Candlelight plays up light and shadows whereas neon is harsh. Most makeup lines advertise the availability of free make-overs throughout the year. These provide a good chance to begin learning basic makeup application. Naturally the purpose of these make-overs is to sell products, and they will use as many as possible on you. Still, at the end of the make-over, you will have had a chance to watch a professional at work. Taking into consideration your own style, you can tailor this information to fit the look that best works for you.

We started with your head; now let's move to your heels. Your shoes should be cleaned and polished. Check them periodically to make sure that the heels have not worn down. Businesspeople make it a habit to pay attention to the condition of your shoes. Experience has taught them that if you are concerned with these types of little details you are a better risk than the person who ignores them.

As you buy clothes, choose styles and colors that will go together. Remember to choose colors that are most flattering to you. There are several books, most of which can be found at the library, which will help you learn the colors best suited for your skin tone. When you go shopping and are tempted to buy a new pair of jeans, stop yourself. Ask if this money wouldn't be better spent on a classic piece of clothing that you could add to your professional wardrobe. After all, you are a very valuable product, and well-packaged products sell the best.

When to Buy

Now that you are dedicated to building your career wardrobe, here are the best months to find good buys on the following items.

Table 1

When to Buy

January	Dresses
	Men's winter clothing
	Men's winter coats
	Men's winter suits
	Women's winter suits
March	Spring clothing
April	Women's coats
	Spring dresses
	Spring suits
June	Dresses
August	Men's & Women's coats
November	Women's coats
	Dresses
	Men's suits

As you can see by this list, there are several times throughout the year to find good buys on the items needed to build a professional wardrobe. By using these guidelines and planning in advance, you will be able to purchase better clothing at more reasonable prices than if you wait until right before graduation.

Before You Buy

Before you begin building your career wardrobe, it is important to take an inventory of the items you already own. Organize your closet by garments and then by color. Do garment checks and make sure each item is in good condition — for example, check for stains, rips, or visible fabric wear. Most important, is the garment the right size? After you have organized your closet, you may be surprised at how many clothes you really have. See how many items you can mix and match to create different outfits. Make sure colors and fabric patterns coordinate when mixing and matching.

Do an inventory of your shoes and handbags, both colors and styles. Next, do an inventory of your undergarments. If these do not fit well, or are in poor condition, it will make a definite difference in how well your outside garments fit and look. Finally, inventory your accessories — scarves, jewelry, etc. Remember, your accessories can give an old outfit a new look.

Table 2

Wardrobe Inventory Checklist — WOMEN

After you have completed your inventories, you will have a better idea of what you will need to complete a beginning wardrobe and set your style.

Item	**Number**	**Colors**
Long-Sleeve Blouses	_____	_____
Short-Sleeve Blouses	_____	_____
Career Tee Shirts	_____	_____
Winter Skirts	_____	_____
Summer Skirts	_____	_____
Dress Pants	_____	_____
Suits	_____	_____
Dresses	_____	_____
Sweaters	_____	_____
Jackets	_____	_____
Blazers	_____	_____
Winter Coats	_____	_____
Purses	_____	_____

Shoes

High Heels	Flats	Boots
_____	_____	_____

Accessories

Scarves	Belts	Jewelry
_____	_____	_____

Chapter 9   **BODY LANGUAGE AND APPEARANCE**

Table 3

Wardrobe Inventory Checklist — MEN

Organize your closet by garments and then by color. Do an inventory of your shoes — styles and colors. Organize ties by color. Socks — make sure you have black. After you have completed your inventories, you will have a better idea of what you will need to complete a beginning wardrobe and set your style.

Item	Number	Colors
Long-Sleeve Shirts	_____	_____
Short-Sleeve Shirts	_____	_____
Dress Slacks	_____	_____
Jackets	_____	_____
Sweaters	_____	_____
Winter Coats	_____	_____
Shoes	_____	_____
Ties	_____	_____
Belts	_____	_____
Socks	_____	_____

Chapter 9

More Steps On My Road To Success
A Personal Review

1. a. What were the key concepts discussed about body language?

   b. What were the key concepts discussed about appearance?

2. How do I plan to put this new body language and appearance knowledge into effect?

3. What are the areas I don't understand or need more information on?

4. What is my game plan for getting the additional information I need?

5. What positive changes do I see in myself?

Chapter 9 Body Language and Appearance

Exercise 1

How well do you present yourself? Use the following questions to conduct an inventory of your personal appearance.

1. Do I usually stand and sit without slouching? _____
2. Is my fragrance light and fresh? _____
3. Are my shoes clean, unscuffed, and presentable? _____
4. Can I quickly find something in my handbag without having to "dig"? _____
5. Are my clothes fresh and free of wrinkles? _____
6. Does my hair need attention no more than once or twice in an eight-hour day? _____
7. Are my hands and fingernails clean and neatly groomed? _____
8. Do I use soap, water, and deodorant to insure good personal hygiene? _____
9. Is my makeup appropriate in both amount and colors? _____
10. Do I dress to flatter my size and build? _____
11. Do I use accessories appropriately? _____
12. Do I choose hose or socks that compliment my outfits? _____
13. Do I wear appropriate undergarments? _____
14. When shopping for clothes, do I choose classics over fads? _____

Chapter 9 Body Language and Appearance

Exercise 2

Charades

1. Your instructor is going to divide you into teams and give each group three 3x5 index cards. Take two minutes and write down on each card an emotion that is shown through body language.

2. At the end of the time limit you will pass the cards back to your instructor, who will then assign them to different teams. At this time, your team will role-play the emotion shown on your card without using words until the other teams guess correctly.

Case Study

Yuriko's Body Language Gets Her in Trouble

When Yuriko arrives at work, she finds a memo stating that her boss wants to hold her annual review at 9:45 a.m. The morning started with a fight with her boyfriend and then her mother, who took the boyfriend's side. The last thing Yuriko wants to do is face the possibility of hearing more criticism. As she enters her supervisor's office, she stares straight ahead, just nodding slightly when she is asked to be seated. As she sits in the large leather chair, she slumps to the left side, crosses her legs, and plays with the four bangle bracelets on her right wrist. Continuing to stare out the window, she answers her boss's questions in a monotone voice.

1. How do you think Yuriko's boss will interpret her actions?

2. What effect will this have on Yuriko's career?

3. How could she more effectively handle this situation?

Remember to take notes during your group discussion of the good ideas developed for future reference.

Suggested Resource Material

Books: Additional Resources

Ludwig, Susan, & Steinberg, Janice. *Petite Style*. NAL-Dutton Publishing Co., 1989.

Head, Sandy Summers. *Sizing Up—Fashion, Fitness & Self Esteem for Full-Figured Women*. Simon & Schuster Publishing Co., 1989.

Molloy, John T. *New Dress for Success*. Warner Books Publishing Co., 1988.

Molloy, John T. *The Woman's Dress for Success Book*. Warner Books Publishing Co., 1984.

Hirschmann, Jane R., & Muntu, Carol. *Overcoming Overeating*. Addison-Wesley Publishing Co., 1988.

Chapter 10

Drug and Alcohol Abuse

"I show my body respect through how I care for it."

Personal Comment Sheet

Entry Date

Five self-positives:

1.

2.

3.

4.

5.

Getting Focused

How do I think the information I am about to read will help me reach my goals?

179

When you first looked over the table of contents for *Creating Your Own Success,* it probably didn't surprise you to see chapters called "Test-Taking Techniques" or "Time Management." It's easy to understand how improving your test-taking skills and using your time wisely will help you succeed. But when you got down to this chapter, "Drug and Alcohol Abuse," you may have felt uneasy. After all, drug and alcohol use are controversial. Some people think alcoholism is a disease. Others blame it on weakness. Some people argue that smoking marijuana should be legal. Others think smoking should be banned all together. No matter how you feel about these issues, even weekend use can limit your career choices after graduation.

"You mean using could really cost me a job?" Yes. Many employers now feel that what you do on your own time is their business. Why do they feel this way? Experience has taught them that employees who use drugs are absent more. They are also less productive when they are present and more likely to injure themselves and other workers. In addition, these high-risk employees cause more damage to equipment. Employers also worry that, due to the expense of their habits, they will steal or involve fellow employees in drugs as a way to make money. The easiest way for employers to avoid these problems is not to hire high-risk employees in the first place.

Because of this change in attitude, when you finish your training you may have to pass a drug test as part of your interview process. The Federal Bureau of Labor statistics estimated in 1991 that more than 145,000 private businesses that employ more than sixteen million people have drug-testing programs. This figure is increasing every day. Since drugs stay in your system, sometimes for months after use has ended, to pass these tests drug use must stop now.

You may have just let out a big sigh of relief because you are not a user. However, don't pat yourself on the back and rush to the next chapter. Even if you don't use, chances are high that substance abuse will touch your life. Because of it, a friend may lose her right to drive. Your boss may begin to act strangely. An elderly relative may begin drinking to ease his loneliness. Why does this behavior start?

Figure 10-1

You may have to pass a drug test as part of your interview process.

Creating Your Own Success

A Hundred and One Reasons

The reasons given for starting drug and alcohol use are as individual as the people themselves. If asked, they might say that their parents allowed them to drink at home to encourage responsibility. Or they might respond that using gave them more energy, helped them lose weight, or helped them relax at parties. In their conversations you might hear them justify their choice by saying that everyone else is doing it. As varied as the reasons are, you can usually fit them into the following categories.

My Friends Talked Me into It

The number one reason people start is peer pressure. Everyone wants to fit in. When we allow others to make us feel different because we don't choose to participate, it makes us uncomfortable. Depending on how high our self-esteem is, we either have the courage to say no or allow others to pressure us into harmful behavior. Anyone who tries to get you to do anything that puts you at risk is NOT a friend and is not worthy of your time. There are no exceptions! If you are experiencing negative peer pressure from the people you presently run around with, then make new friends. Where should you look for these positive friends? How about considering the people that are in your classroom right now?

It's OK to Take Stuff to Feel Better

John wakes up with a headache, so before leaving for work he pops two pain relievers. At his ten o'clock break he notices that his stomach is burning from the pills he took this morning, so he downs two caps of antacid. Around three o'clock he decides that he feels so lousy because he is coming down with a cold. Right away he takes two cold tablets and some cough syrup. John's reaction to not feeling well is fairly typical.

We have grown up in a society in which if you don't feel good you take something to make you feel better. People think nothing of mentioning that they need a cup of coffee or caffeine soft drink to help them get going in the morning. When the newspapers report about a possible new diet drug that will help us lose weight, we read on with eager anticipation. Watching TV bombards our subconscious with advertisements encouraging us to take products to feel better. It's not hard to understand how, in this environment, some people cross the line from use to abuse.

It Looked Like a Good Idea

We've all seen the ads showing the gorgeous bikini-clad models draped over the skinny guy because he was holding the "right" brew. By high school graduation a person has seen an average of 100,000 of these commercials. And what message do these ads send? They show us that alcohol is a fun and harmless part of every social function. We also receive these types of messages from movies, music, and some of our friends. We may even receive these messages from our family.

Marcos and his dad love football. During the season they watch games together all day Saturday and Sunday. As they sit in front of the TV, his dad drinks a couple of beers. He says they help him relax and with his high-stress job he's earned them. What message is Marcos's dad sending him?

Marcy and her friends go to the opening of a new movie. The movie contains several scenes showing the lead female, a gorgeous former model, at dinner and at parties. In each of these scenes she has just secretly used cocaine. Not only is she having lots of fun, but she also has the attention of every male present. As Marcy watches the movie, she thinks about how plain she is by comparison and how much she would like to be like the woman on the screen. What messages could Marcy get from this movie? She could leave the theater thinking that drug use would make her more fun and therefore more desirable. Or she could decide to find other ways to feel better about herself — for example, a new make-over or exercise program. If she decides that drugs and alcohol are not a good idea, what steps can she take to help her say no?

Learning to Say No

Saying no is not always easy. When a friend hands us a drink, we may feel foolish refusing it. When we go to a party and see drugs being used, we may feel out of touch. We may even catch ourselves envying the fun they seem to be having. The more pressure we feel to participate the more important it is to learn to cope with peer pressure, be assertive, relax, and raise our self-esteem.

Increasing Your Self-Esteem

The higher your self-approval rating the easier it will be for you to say no to situations and options that you feel uncomfortable with. If you already feel good about yourself, congratulations. That is no small accomplishment in a society that loves to point out all the things we need to fix. But what if your self-esteem is low?

Trina grew up in a household where she almost never received a compliment. Instead of being proud of her accomplishments, her parents always expected her to do more. As an adult Trina has grown to realize that just because she grew up with low self-esteem doesn't mean she has to keep feeling that way. Though at first it felt silly, she is increasing her self-esteem by giving herself several honest compliments daily. As she gets dressed for school, she looks in the mirror and compliments herself on the results she is seeing from her exercise program. In her typing class she reaches a new speed level and silently tells herself that she is proud of this achievement. Besides these compliments, at the end of every day she writes in a special diary. On these pages she only records what she did right that day and those areas where she sees progress. Sitting on the edge of her bed, she enters how great it feels to reach her new typing speed. Next, she writes how proud she is that her clothes are fitting better with her new diet and exercise program.

This diary not only helps her feel better now, but when she has a tough day she can increase her feelings of self-worth by reading her past entries.

Just like Trina, you can raise your confidence level by learning and practicing new skills. Take a second now to think about how good it feels when you successfully do something new for the first time. Whether it is repairing an airplane engine, programing a computer, balancing a ledger sheet, or leading a discussion group in this class, it feels great. Every positive experience you have adds to your feeling of self-worth. Another way to increase your self-esteem is to eat right and exercise. As your energy level and stamina increase, you will begin to see yourself in a more favorable light.

Like Trina, Kana grew up with low self-esteem. He comes from a large family where each child had to fend for him- or herself. His parents loved him, but they just didn't have much time to show it. To get attention he began to get in trouble and even spent the night in jail. That experience convinced him he needed to make a change. Since he realized he could not change his parents, he decided to work on his self-acceptance. Talking with his school counselor brought out several issues. She helped Kana be aware that he had always felt bad about himself because he did not make the football team like his older brothers. This helped explain part of the reason his self-esteem was low. He continually downplayed his talents because he felt they didn't stack up against his brothers'. With his counselor's help he learned to stop competing with other people and to start keying in on his own abilities. She also showed him how to develop his thinking skills so that he could make better decisions and stay out of trouble.

Improving Your Thinking Skills

Just like Kana, everybody thinks. But some people do it more effectively than others. What secrets do these "better thinkers" have?

Beth has learned from experience that there is a big difference between a fact and an opinion. She knows it is a fact that marijuana contains 426 different chemicals. When Owen tries to convince her that smoking marijuana is harmless, she knows that is just his opinion. And she isn't about to make her decisions based on an opinion.

Nakisha is open to new ideas and doesn't argue when she knows nothing about the subject. Instead she listens to the other person, checks out the facts, and then makes up her own mind. She is never afraid to question things that don't make sense. And she works to build her vocabulary so she can understand other people's ideas and express her own more effectively.

When Levi was a little boy, he asked many questions. His mother responded by telling him to shut up. If he questioned why she wanted him to do something, she always said, "Because I told you to." After a while he quit asking questions at all. Now when his friends tell him something, it never enters his mind to wonder if they are right. His friend Nina has been telling him how much fun it is to get high. He wants her to like him so he plans to join in next time she does cocaine. What thinking skills could Levi learn from Nakisha and Beth to help him make a good decision?

Learning to Cope with Peer Pressure

What is peer pressure? It is what Levi is experiencing from Nina. When we allow our desire to be accepted by other people to influence our actions, this is peer pressure. The necktie is a good example of peer pressure. Neckties serve no purpose, but peer pressure dictates that businessmen wear them if they want to fit in. Not all peer pressure is negative. If you are a member of a study group, you probably challenge each other to work hard. This is a positive form of peer pressure.

Eloisa has just gotten an invitation to attend a party given by one of her oldest friends. Concerned that Doresha runs with a wilder crowd than when they first met, Eloisa has a decision to make. She has heard through the grapevine that the last party Doresha sponsored got out of hand. Rather than waiting until the party to decide what to say or how to act if offered drugs, she is going to develop an action plan now. With her sister's help, she role-plays different ways she can handle this situation. What types of statements could Eloisa make?

She can say no and give a reason for her refusal. "No, I don't choose to do cocaine because I know it is bad for me" makes it clear that she knows the facts and is not going to change her mind. But what if she would be uncomfortable making such a strong statement? Then she can simply say "No thanks" and walk away. Or she can say, "Thanks, but I think I'll get a soft drink instead." When you develop your own refusal statements, it is best to keep them clear and simple. You do not have to explain your reasons if you do not want to.

As the date of the party gets closer, Eloisa begins to think about another option. Realizing that she cannot please everyone, she decides that her commitment to her own success is more important than her friendship with Doresha. Well aware that it may mean the end of an old friendship, she decides that for her, the best plan of action is not to attend. By avoiding the situation she can insure that she does not give in to peer pressure. Instead of just sitting home that night, she makes plans to go to a movie with some of her success network friends. By taking this positive step, Eloisa will prevent herself from sitting around and feeling sorry over the possible loss of an old friend. Instead she can focus on developing a long-term relationship with people who will add to her self-esteem and personal growth. Can you pick out the positive steps Eloisa took to handle peer pressure?

First, she decided before the party that she planned to stay substance-free. She did not wait to make such an important

Creating Your Own Success

decision until she was in the middle of the party. Next, role-playing with her sister allowed her to practice a variety of responses until they felt natural. Most of us can express our thoughts more effectively if we have time to plan what we are going to say. After thinking about the party, Eloisa decided that the best way to remain substance-free was to avoid situations where they would be present. This may not be the choice she makes every time. Sometimes it may not even be possible. For example, her job may require her to attend a company function where alcohol is served. Before attending any such events, she can again practice her refusal statements. Eventually, as she gains more experience, her responses and behavior will come naturally.

As Eloisa gains more life experiences, it may surprise her to find that handling peer pressure is difficult whether you are nineteen or fifty-five. This is true because the desire to fit in never leaves us. Since we will experience these feelings throughout life, it is a good idea to have a variety of responses. What are other methods we can use to cope with peer pressure?

Figure 10-2

Our desire to fit in makes handling peer pressure difficult.

Laimute E. Druskis/Stock, Boston

When you are in a negative peer pressure situation, ask yourself, "What price am I willing to pay to be popular with these people?" As you think about this question, some important issues will come to mind. Are you willing to risk your health? Your freedom? Your job? The loss of their friendship? Are they really your friends to begin with? And do you want them to be? As we said at the start of this chapter, real friends do not try to get you to do anything that may harm you. As Eloisa learned, you can't please everybody. Even when the peer pressure you experience is positive, it's a good idea to decide for yourself whether following their advice or example is in your best interest.

Learning to Be Assertive

Chanda was taught never to talk back. Out of habit she keeps her eyes focused on the floor and talks in a soft voice. When people try to pressure her into things, although she says no, they don't give up. Sick of not being taken seriously, she decides to change the way she communicates. At the library she reads everything she can find about being assertive. When she finishes, she understands why people don't take her seriously.

In the past she has defended her decisions and sometimes even gone as far as apologizing for them. To be assertive, she is going to have to learn to make eye contact, use a firm, strong voice, and say no like she means it. After practicing on her own, she talks her sister into helping her strengthen these new skills. Over the next several days, they spend time role-playing a variety of situations. After two weeks of practice, she feels very comfortable with her new responses.

Walking back from the park, Misha spots Chanda and decides to have some fun. Catching up to her, she asks Chanda to a party she is going to have while her parents are out of town. Describing all of the wildness at her last party, Misha raises an eyebrow when Chanda does not turn her usual bright shade of red. She is even more surprised by the fact that Chanda is making direct eye contact.

As Chanda listens, she decides that now is as good a time as any to practice her new skills. In a clear, strong voice she says, "Thanks for the invitation, but that's not for me. I understand why you asked me. In the past I have allowed you to embarrass me. I don't choose to do that any more." Leaving Misha with a shocked look on her face, Chanda heads for home with a triumphant smile. What can you learn from Chanda's example?

Learning to Relax

Remember the relaxation technique we discussed in Chapter 8? This can help you pass more than just a test. Learning to use relaxation techniques can help you avoid the use of drugs or alcohol to reduce your stress levels. It can also help you if you are in a relationship where there is substance abuse. There are many methods you can use besides the one we covered in Chapter 8. For example, next time you feel your stress level rising, stop what you are doing, sit if possible, and take three or four slow, deep breaths. This will slow your heart rate and help you feel calmer.

Derrick has just moved back in with his parents. Having been away two years, he had forgotten how stressful it was to live at home. When she gets home from work every night, his mother starts drinking vodka. His father pretends that this is not happening by blaming her slowed speech and unsteady walk on tiredness. After two weeks of feeling the pressure build, Derrick starts using some relaxation techniques. He also makes sure to talk with his support group weekly. It doesn't embarrass him to admit that he can't handle his situation alone. His group helps him reduce his stress by pointing out that it is impossible to please everyone. They also help him write out a coping statement that he can repeat to himself when he feels the pressure increasing. At first he questions the effectiveness of saying, "I can deal with this until graduation." But after a few days of practice, he sees that his coping statement is helping. In addition, they help him understand the difference between use and abuse.

How Do I Know If It's Use or Abuse?

The first thing to remember is not to jump to conclusions. People's behavior can change for a variety of reasons. For example, a person may act differently because of working overtime, a fight with a spouse, an adverse reaction to prescription medicine, or low or high blood sugar. The important thing to keep in mind is that these clues are not a signal for accusations. Instead, try to involve the other person in a conversation so you can learn more.

Alcohol

In our example, Derrick is dealing with a tough situation. He thinks his mother abuses alcohol. His father denies that this is a problem and his mother points to the fact that she holds a responsible position without any problem. But just because a person can hold a job or function in society doesn't mean that person does not have a problem with alcohol. How can Derrick tell if his mother has crossed the narrow line between user and abuser?

Here are a few of the areas he can look at. Does she use a drink as a crutch, pouring herself one when faced with a problem? Can she stop herself or, after one drink, does she keep going until she becomes intoxicated? Has it affected her work performance or attendance? Would either of these areas have been affected if his father had not stepped in and covered for her? Does she drive after drinking? Does she use every excuse as a reason to celebrate, with alcohol being an important part of the party? Has she ever bragged about how much she can drink before it affects her?

If Derrick answered yes to several of these questions it doesn't mean his mother is an alcoholic, but it does mean that her drinking is out of control.

Other Drugs

Dani has always taken a great deal of pride in her looks and grades. Before this semester she was president of her honor society, involved in the data processing club, and an active volunteer at an area animal shelter. However, since she began dating Garrett all this has changed. Now she misses school frequently and when she does show up is unprepared. When Larell, her best friend, runs into her on campus he can't believe the change. She has lost too much weight and is wearing baggy, wrinkled clothes. When he tries to talk with her, she is hostile and uses language he has never heard from her before. Laughing off his concerns, she asks him for money, breaking off eye contact when he wants to know what it's for. Without thanking him, she grabs the twenty from his hand and runs for the pay phone. Watching her talk happily on the phone, he tries to tell himself that he is overreacting to the changes he sees in Dani. Do you agree?

Dani has given Larell some definite clues to her drug use. What are they? Her abrupt mood changes and poor attendance all point to possible substance abuse. An increase in family problems, temper flare-ups, and an increased need for money can also signal trouble. If the person gets more secretive, hangs around with a different group of friends, and changes his or her language and behavior, substance abuse may be the reason. Can you spot the other clues Dani sent? Once Larell and Derrick accept that someone they care about may be a substance abuser, what should they do?

Toward Recovery

In the past twenty years the options for people who are abusers and the people who care for them have grown greatly. Now there are support groups and programs for just about every type of addiction you can think of, from alcohol to gambling. Support and help are available even if your addiction is food. No matter what the addiction, it affects the lives of not only the abuser but also those around him or her.

If the Abuser Is You

It's pretty clear that Larell and Derrick cannot force the people they care about to change. If Derrick's mom wants to change, she must take the first step by admitting that she has a problem. Dani must do the same thing. Neither of them will see the need for help if they continue to deny that they are substance abusers.

If you feel that you may have a problem with substance abuse, you will also need to take this first step. This is not necessarily easy. But the good news is, you don't have to do it alone. There are many people just like you who have taken this first step and are willing to help you do the same. How do you find them? In the resource section of this chapter we have included several organizations that specialize in a variety of substance-abuse areas. They will be glad to put you in touch with the group in your area. Or you can locate some of them in the Yellow Pages under the listing for Alcoholism Information & Treatment Centers. Though the title suggests only information on alcoholism, this is a good place to start for any drug problem. These people will be glad to confidentially direct you to programs for other addictions. If you feel comfortable with your instructor or another member of the staff, you may also wish to ask for their help and support.

Once you admit that you need help, how do you decide which group or treatment center is right for you? Look for a group or center that you feel comfortable with. No matter how highly recommended they are, if you don't feel they will be supportive of you then they are not a good choice. Don't get discouraged. Just keep looking. When you do find an environment that is supportive and positive, make sure that they will help you strengthen your communication, decision-making, and problem-solving skills. In addition, they should have a plan that will help you increase your self-esteem, get your family involved in the treatment process, and offer long-term support.

If the Abuser Is Someone You Care About

Just like Larell and Derrick, you do not have it in your power to change an abuser. The only thing you can change is how you choose to deal with his or her behavior. As we said before, it is best not to jump to conclusions. Try to get the person to talk with you and keep in mind that you cannot replace a trained drug and alcohol counselor. Your role is to be a friend and good example. Be willing to listen to them talk about why they choose to do drugs while being firm in your explanation of why this use is hurting them. Offer to help them find someone who can help them kick their habit and provide the moral support they may need to make that first contact. Follow up with them, praising each positive step they take. Although it is hard, try not to show disappointment if they stumble back into old habits.

If they should revert to old ways, continue being a friend but do not cover their behavior for them or make excuses. By making excuses for his wife, Derrick's father is not helping her. Instead, his behavior is enabling her to continue denying that she has a problem. What are other things enablers do? They may call and request a sick day for the abuser, flush their drugs down the drain, or continually buy into their excuses for being late to work or broke. These acts do not help the person take responsibility for his or her actions. Covering their substance abuse for them only hurts them in the long run.

What are other things you should not do? It is a good idea to refrain from sarcasm, accusations, or seeking sympathy for yourself and your own troubles. Try not to fall into the trap of using emotional appeals. For example, asking your spouse to think about your children may only increase his or her guilt and lead to more abuse. In addition, it is not wise to discuss their abuse when they are under the influence of drugs or alcohol.

Aisha and Bill have been together for five years. Although it is hard, Aisha has finally accepted that Bill is a substance abuser. She has read a lot about abuse and is no longer an enabler. But even with this knowledge, she feels very frustrated and alone. The way he acts when under the influence makes her feel ashamed. She no longer wants to go anywhere with him and allows this to make her feel guilty. She also wonders if she hasn't in some way added to the problem. At lunch she hears one of her co-workers talking about support groups that help people who are in codependent relationships. Back in her office, she looks through the white pages for the name of the group she heard mentioned. Her hand shakes as she dials their number. After two rings she begins to hang up. But before the handset reaches the cradle, she hears a friendly voice saying hello. Swallowing hard, she returns the handset to her ear and asks for help.

It was not easy for Aisha to reach out for help and support. But just as this is the first step for the abuser, it is also the first step for his or her family and friends. There are many excellent programs that can help deal with the feelings that you experience in a codependent relationship. We have included a list of places to contact in the resource section of this chapter. Or you can look in the Yellow Pages under Alcoholism and Treatment Centers. The questions to ask before joining a group are much the same as those listed under the "If the Abuser Is You" section. The most important thing to remember is that you do not need to be brave or deal with this on your own. Help is available, and it is a sign of strength to reach out for it. As you begin to understand yourself better and how you have allowed this person's behavior to affect your life, you will begin to feel healthier. This may mean a change in, or end to, this relationship. It is possible that when the user sees your progress, he or she may also reach for help. But no matter what choices the other person makes, you will be dealing with life as a responsible person and not a victim. There are also many excellent books, some of which we have listed, that can help you during this transition. Through reading you can strengthen your resolve, increase your knowledge, and weather this storm stronger than ever.

Chapter 10

More Steps On My Road To Success
A Personal Review

1. What key concepts were discussed about drug and alcohol abuse?

2. How do I plan to put this new knowledge into effect?

3. What are the areas I don't understand or need more information on?

4. What is my game plan for getting the additional information I need?

5. What positive changes do I see in myself?

Chapter 10 Drug and Alcohol Abuse

Exercise 1

1. Research which major employers in your area are doing drug testing and what kind of test they are using.

2. Find out how drug tests work and what some of the complications are. How are legal prescription drugs and over-the-counter medicines handled?

3. Research which major employers in your area offer Employee Assistance Programs.

4. In class, share and discuss the information you have learned. Talk about how it will affect your employment options.

Chapter 10   Drug and Alcohol Abuse

Exercise 2

1. Write out a list of things that your friends or family pressure you to do.

2. Is this positive peer pressure or negative? Why?

3. Using what you learned from this chapter, what do you need to do to increase your self-esteem, and strengthen your coping and thinking skills?

4. How will this action help you deal with negative peer pressure?

5. Finish these statements.
   I feel strong when I _____
   _____

   I felt good about myself when _____
   _____

   I feel independent when _____
   _____

6. When someone tries to pressure me into doing something I am not comfortable with, I will use the following assertive statements to express myself:

Chapter 6   Time Management

Exercise 3

Bring in or describe an example of how the media (TV, newspaper, magazine, radio) encourages or discourages drug use. Be prepared to talk about your example as part of a group discussion.

Case Study

Alfonso's Choices

Alfonso has worked hard to stay sober over the last year by regularly attending Alcoholics Anonymous meetings and by avoiding situations that might tempt him. After being on the job only one week, he begins to hear plans for the annual year-end Ledger Closing party. Asking one of his co-workers about this event, he learns that his supervisor, Tom, will host it at a local bar. Concerned, Alfonso returns to his desk and begins to consider his options.

1. List the options that Alfonso has, showing the pluses and minuses for each.

2. Which option do you recommend he choose and why?

Suggested Resource Material

Books: Additional Resources

The book *Let's All Work to Fight Drug Abuse* offers excellent information on drugs and alcohol. It also explains their effects on individuals and families. It is distributed by:
L.A.W. Publications
4213 Wiley Post Road, Suite 100
Addison, TX 75244
(214) 387-2230

Kokin, Morris, & Walker, Ian. *Women Married to Alcoholics.* Morrow Books Publishing Co., 1989.

Siegel, Ronald K., Ph.D. *Intoxication.* Pocket Books Publishing Co., 1990.

Ackerman, Robert J. *Children of Alcoholics.* Simon & Schuster Publishing Co., 1987.

Walker, Richmond. *The 7 Points of Alcoholic Anonymous.* Glen Abbey Books Publishing Co., 1987.

Muney, Jack. *Loving an Alcoholic.* Bantam Books Publishing Co., 1988.

Millham, Peter, & Mason, Bruce. *The White Book—A Guide to Addiction Recovery.* Beacon Books Publishing Co., 1989.

Beattie, Melody. *Codependent: No More.* Harper & Collins Publishing Co., 1989.

DuPont, Robert L., Jr. *Getting Tough on Gateway Drugs: A Guide for the Family.* American Psychiatric Press Inc., 1985.

Norris, Charles R., Jr. *Family Addictions: A Guide for Surviving Alcohol & Drug Abuse.* PIA Publishing Co., 1990.

Hostetler, Jeb. *Ten Things Parents Should Know About Drug & Alcohol Abuse.* Good Books Publishing Co., 1991.

For Literature on Cocaine and Other Drugs:

American Council for Drug Education
204 Monroe Street
Rockville, MD 20850
(301)294-0600

National Federation of Parents for Drug-Free Youth
8730 Georgia Avenue, Suite 200
Silver Spring, MD 20910
1-800-554-KIDS (301)585-5437

ORGANIZATIONS: ADDITIONAL RESOURCES

If you are an abuser . . .

Alcoholics Anonymous World Services
P.O. Box 459
Grand Central Station
New York, NY 10017

Overeaters Anonymous World Service Office
P.O. Box 92870
Los Angeles, CA 90009

Anorexics/Bulimics Anonymous
P.O. Box 112214
San Diego, CA 92111

Gamblers Anonymous
P.O. Box 17173
Los Angeles, CA 90017

Smokers Anonymous
2118 Greenwich St.
San Francisco, CA 94123

If the abuser is someone you care about . . .

CoDa-Teen (part of Codependents Anonymous)
P.O. Box 33577
Phoenix, AZ 85067

Codependents Anonymous
P.O. Box 35577
Phoenix, AZ 85067

Al-Anon (for families of alcoholics)
P.O. Box 862
Midtown Station
New York, NY 10018
800-356-9996

Adult Children of Alcoholics
P.O. Box 3216
2522 W. Sepulveda Blvd.
Suite 200
Torrance, CA 90505

Nar-Anon (for families of drug addicts)
P.O. Box 2562
Palos Verdes, CA 90274

Gam-Anon (for families of compulsive gamblers)
P.O. Box 157
Whitestone, NY 11357

If in looking over either of these lists, you do not see a group you feel can help, contact:

>   National Self-Help Clearing House
>   25 West 43rd St.
>   Room 620
>   New York, NY 10036

Chapter 11
Relationships

"Relationships are like my checking account. I have to remember to put in as much as I take out."

Personal Comment Sheet

Entry Date

Five self-positives:

1.

2.

3.

4.

5.

Getting Focused

How do I think the information I am about to read will help me reach my goals?

We spend all of our lives around other people. Yet to many of us, our relationships are a mystery. We get along with some people, we don't with others. We talk about chemistry and kindred spirits as if good relationships were based on magic. But when it comes to bad relationships we know just where to place the blame. With quick-draw fingers, we can point to all of the other person's flaws, each shortcoming described in vivid detail. Is it our fate to be surrounded by people, yet unable through our own actions to change the relationships we have with them?

No. By learning to communicate more clearly, accept change, and show appreciation, we can all benefit from stronger, healthier relationships.

Figure 11-1

Most relationships begin with communication.

Communication

Most relationships begin with communication, endure because of communication, and often end because of the lack of communication. Communication works best when it is a two-sided affair. However, the only person you can really control in a relationship is yourself. You can't make others communicate if they do not wish to. It is also wise to remember that actions often speak louder than words.

Kevin and Kenisha have been friends for over two years. Kevin has caught Kenisha in several lies and gets angry when she nags him about getting a better job. Kenisha lies to Kevin because he is jealous of the time she spends with her friends studying and she wants to avoid a fight. When they do fight, she brings up all the gossip she heard about him from his old girlfriend, and he hurts her back by bringing up the fact that she has gained weight since they met. After several days of not speaking to him, Kenisha gets tired of being alone and always ends up finding a reason to invite him over. To avoid having to talk about the fight, they always celebrate getting back together by going to a noisy restaurant and movie. Happy until the next time, they settle into their

200 **Creating Your Own Success**

regular routine. Can you spot the communication mistakes Kevin and Kenisha are making?

Face Facts

Rather than dealing with the fact of Kevin's jealousy, Kenisha is choosing to lie. You cannot solve problems in a relationship if you are not willing to face them. That is why lying is always a bad choice. Good relationships, whether they are between family members, friends, or co-workers, are based on openness and honesty. By complicating matters with untruths, Kenisha now has two problems instead of just one. She has to deal with the fact that Kevin does not trust her to tell the truth and also his jealousy. Instead of avoiding facing his jealousy, she would be better off trying to discuss with him why he feels jealous. After she listens to his comments, she can try to explain how his accusations make her feel. If this is done calmly as soon as the issue surfaces, there is a much better chance that each party will be willing to listen to the other.

How should Kenisha go about starting this discussion? By waiting until they are alone, relaxed, and have time to thoroughly cover the issue, she is giving them the best chance to solve their problems. Sometimes this is hard to do. When something comes up, we want to jump right in. But if we choose a time when the other person is in a hurry or distracted, we have already set ourselves up for possible failure.

After Kenisha picks the best time, she should open the discussion by describing the problem as she views it without placing blame or making accusations. A simple statement like, "Kevin, something has been bothering me and I'd like to talk it over with you. When I study with my friends, it seems to make you jealous. I react to this by feeling uncomfortable and defensive. Can we talk about how you feel when I study with my friends?" By telling Kevin what she has been experiencing in a non-threatening way, she stands a better chance of learning why he reacts the way he does. Until they each understand how the other feels and why, they cannot work toward a solution. As they begin to share their feelings, they should each admit to any ways in which they have contributed to the problem. When Kevin says he only became concerned when he stopped by and she wasn't there and then later told him she was, she should take responsibility for her actions, and then explain the reason for them. As the discussion continues they should begin to look for common ground and possible solutions. Before they end their discussion, they should agree upon a plan of action that will begin to solve the problem.

Watch Your Words

Both Kevin and Kenisha need to be more aware of what they say. Instead of nagging him about getting a better job, she should try to be supportive. By taking the time to listen to why he likes the job he has, she may learn something. Also, if he feels she is willing to listen he may be less defensive. Every relationship is going to have to work through problems. By sharing the problem, suggesting solutions, and looking for ways to work together, rather than nagging or griping, each party will enjoy the relationship more.

What about Kevin's comment about Kenisha's weight? When we are mad, it is easy to verbally hit below the belt. A relationship requires that each party reveal facts about themselves and in most instances the deeper the relationship the more intimate the facts become. This kind of knowledge gives us all the ammunition we need to hurt each other. It is tempting to say, "If you loved me you would . . ." or "You're just like that bum you have for a father." The only thing this type of fighting accomplishes is a lot of bad feeling and broken relationships. Instead, make sure that you keep the discussion centered on the issues at hand.

Stick to the Issues

In our example Kevin and Kenisha need to talk about his jealousy and her dissatisfaction with his job. All the other issues they are bringing up in their fights only distract them from dealing with the real problems. By tossing his old girlfriend into the fight, Kenisha is trying to distract Kevin from talking about her lying or how he feels about her nagging. Instead of bringing up the past, Kenisha could choose to strengthen their relationship by taking responsibility for her actions and discussing why she chose to lie in the first place. Instead of bringing up her weight gain, Kevin could talk about how he feels when he finds out she is lying.

Romance the World

When we first start a relationship, it is common for us to find everything this new person says fascinating. When we are around them we want to look our best, and we treat them with extra special care. After time goes on and the novelty wears off, we forget to extend these little courtesies. We assume that because we've known them a while we can say whatever is on our mind without any filtering. By this time we think we know them better than they do themselves, so we can interpret their actions without asking them and finish their sentences. This allows us to ignore most of what they say. When we do pay attention, because we care about them, we give them the benefit of our good advice, whether they have asked for it or not. Over time the relationship loses its glow or dies altogether. How do we prevent this from happening?

We need to romance each other. Forget that we usually think about romance in terms of an intimate relationship; think about how most of us act at the start of a romance. We are kind, generous of spirit, gentle with each other's feelings, and willing to ignore each other's flaws. We take extra care to look and act our best so that the other person will enjoy being around us. We listen carefully, offer supportive comments, and keep our promises. Our greatest wish is for the other person to be happy and well. We wish for them what we wish for ourselves. We treat them as we would like to be treated. If you make this last sentence your guiding principle in dealing with others, your side of the relationship will be healthy and strong.

Change

It is not within Kevin's power to change Kenisha, just as it is not in Kenisha's power to change Kevin. You can only work to make your side of any relationship healthy and strong. What if Kevin follows our advice and starts communicating effectively but Kenisha does not choose to change? Kevin can either accept Kenisha as she is or decide that it is not healthy for him to have a relationship with her. Many people stay in relationships that are unhealthy because they are not willing to see that these are the only two choices. Instead, they either hope for a miracle or begin to enjoy their status as a martyr. They are willing to accept inevitable unhappiness rather than face the unknown.

Why would someone make this choice? Because they are afraid of change. But change in life is inevitable. As you get older your body will change; when you graduate from school, your job opportunities will change; if you have children, as they grow up your relationship with them will change. Change is part of life and will happen whether you want it to or not. So instead of being afraid of it, learn to accept and adjust to it. How do you do this? By learning to understand the three steps most people encounter when dealing with change.

Endings

Every change begins with an ending. Feeling pain or anger during this stage is natural. Though these endings may be painful, they are nothing to be afraid of. As you experience an ending, take time each day to concentrate on the good that is going to come from this change. With every ending there is new opportunity.

Acceptance

Time is a great healer. Eventually you move through the pain or anger, leaving the past behind and looking toward the future. This time between endings and beginnings is always a necessary step. During this step you should examine both the positive and negative aspects of the relationship and learn from the lessons that this introspective examination will reveal. It is important that you accept responsibility for choosing to participate in the relationship and learn how to make healthier choices in the future. You do not learn by blaming yourself or others. Only by honestly looking at the part you played in the relationship and changing any negative behavior can you hope to move on to better relationships.

New Beginnings

There are no endings without new beginnings, or new beginnings without endings. Use wisdom in starting your new beginnings. Always look at all of your options.

When you are experiencing change, it is important to communicate with those around you. If they see you behaving differently, with new goals and positive habits, but you never tell them why these changes are important to you, then they will feel lost and shut out. This is a good example of why clear, honest communication is the foundation for good relationships.

Appreciation

Let those important people in your life know just how important they really are. List these important people and all the ways each has contributed and influenced your life. Acknowledge them through letters, calls, visits. Thank them for touching your life. Showing your appreciation to others is the sweet cement that helps to reinforce relationships.

We Are All Just People

Cultural diversity is a popular new phrase that you may have seen or heard used by the news media. Though the words may sound kind of intimidating, all they really mean is that as a group we will all be stronger if we accept and appreciate the differences we bring to our world. In the past we thought of ourselves as a "melting pot" where people from all other countries and lifestyles came to America. Giving up the traditions of their native lands, they learned our language, our styles, and over a period of time "melted" into our society. Now we are seeing that when we bring the strengths of all of our different backgrounds into society without diluting them it makes us stronger by allowing us to draw on a wider variety of knowledge.

Figure 11-2

We have a culturally diverse society.

Of course this transition, from expecting everyone to act and think pretty much alike to our present goal of enjoying both the things that make us different and alike, is not always easy. Many people have been raised to have preconceived notions about groups of people. Some people really believe that women are too emotional to be in positions of power, or that African-Americans are better athletes without effort, and some amuse themselves by portraying Polish people as stupid. What other prejudices can you think of that either you have or aware of? When we lump people together like this, it is called stereotyping.

204   Creating Your Own Success

Getting Beyond Stereotypes

How do we move beyond these prejudiced stereotypes? First, when you are introduced to someone for the first time, if you catch yourself making judgments about them, immediately interrupt your brain and ask it for specific facts to back up these thoughts. Since you will not have had time to make a fact-based judgment on this person yet, the information you are filtering into your brain is probably based on stereotypes. If you find yourself still lumping people together, take a look at your own family. Your family shares a common history, but even with this you are totally unique, just like the person in front of you. Just like you, they have their own set of experiences, beliefs, and ideas; though they may be similar, they are not like anyone you have ever met before.

As you continue your conversation with them, concentrate on all the things you have in common: same sex, both right-handed, love clothes, or having trouble in English class. After you have taken note of what is the same, learn about your differences. You will find that once you are no longer burdened by preconceived notions, life will be more interesting because, rather than assuming what a person or group is like, you will give them the chance to show you. Shutting ourselves off from these experiences by insisting on only being with or listening to "our own kind" is fortunately no longer an option. We all need the skills, traditions, and unique backgrounds that we, as a culturally diverse country, bring to the future. It starts with each of us, now.

Relationships That Hurt: Being Battered

Although most of the victims of this type of abuse are women, do not assume that this is always the case. Men too can find themselves in relationships where they are the object of mental or physical abuse. There are a few simple things to remember about these types of abuse.

If you are physically or mentally abusive, you need professional help. Your behavior is NOT acceptable and is harmful to both the person you are abusing and to you. Do not wait until the "next time" to get help. Do it now. Your instructor or the college counselor can refer you to people that want to help you. Through classes and counseling you can learn to control yourself and have healthy relationships. You deserve to feel better about yourself. There is no shame in a hand reaching for help, only a closed fist.

If you are being physically or mentally abused, only you have the power to stop it. The first step is to accept the fact that no one, not even you, deserves this type of treatment. Physical or mental abuse is NEVER deserved or acceptable. You must take action to end this abuse by reaching out to your instructors, the college counselor, and your area abuse services. There are a lot of people willing to help, but ONLY you can take the first steps to recovering your life.

Sexual Harassment

How do you know if you are being sexually harassed? If you are the object of behavior with unwelcome sexual overtones or of a sexual nature, you are being harassed. This includes, but is not limited to, remarks, jokes, touching, or coercion based on promotions or job security. When we think of sexual harassment, we usually think of the man as being the perpetrator, but that is not always the case. As more and more women enter power positions, they too can be guilty of sexual harassment.

If you feel that you are being sexually harassed then there are some important steps you need to take. First, you must be sure to state your feelings clearly so that there is no doubt that you do not like the harassing actions or words. Simple statements like "Stop, I don't like what you are doing," "I do not wish to see you outside of work hours," "When you make sexual remarks or tell jokes it makes me uncomfortable," or "Please stop" get your message across clearly. In addition to sending this type of verbal signal, don't forget the importance of body language. By keeping your arms folded, making your face match the seriousness of your words, or even pushing someone away if necessary, you are backing up your statement that the behavior is unwelcome.

Another step that is important is to document these instances of harassment by taking notes or keeping a log. If you should choose to pursue this further, written documentation will help it from becoming a case of just your word against your harasser's. Finally, if you have stated clearly that you feel their behavior constitutes sexual harassment and the behavior continues, report it to the correct official of your organization or your local Equal Employment Opportunity office. Before you take these last steps, evaluate your own behavior and make sure that your actions in no way could have been interpreted to have welcomed this type of behavior. That is why it is important to shine in both professional behavior and appearance so that your actions do not draw unwanted attention. Think of it as defensive driving. Sure, the other driver should be operating his or her automobile correctly, but we all know it doesn't always work that way. Part of the responsibility falls on us to make sure that accidents don't happen. Take time to think in advance if an outfit, joke, or late-night hours might set up a situation that you don't want. A little caution up front may save a lot of trouble later on.

Chapter 11

More Steps On My Road To Success
A Personal Review

1. What were the key concepts discussed about relationships?

2. How do I plan to put this new relationship knowledge into effect?

3. What are the areas I don't understand or need more information on?

4. What is my game plan for getting the additional information I need?

5. What positive changes do I see in myself?

Chapter 11   Relationships

Exercise 1

Using what you have learned in this chapter, write a positive dialogue for the following situations.

1. Shauna and Sonia have been roommates for three years. During this time Sonia has always borrowed Shauna's clothes without asking. Unwilling to confront Sonia, Shauna has always let it pass — until tonight when she sees Sonia in the very dress she had planned to wear to the company Christmas party. Write an example of a positive discussion Shauna could have with Sonia.

2. Mr. Longston always gives his employees last-minute assignments that force them to work late. Usually Joe can overlook this, but tonight is his son's first school play. As a single father, Joe feels he has to be there. As Mr. Longston approaches his desk with two thick file folders in his hands, Joe tries to come up with a positive way to tell Mr. Longston that he can't stay. Write an example of a positive discussion Joe could have with Mr. Longston.

Chapter 11 Relationships

Exercise 2

Think about one of your relationships in which communication isn't working — brother, friend, lover, boss, or spouse. Next, list everything that bugs you about the relationship. After listing all the things that bother you, list all the ways you may have contributed to the problem. Finally, select which of the guidelines you can use to help improve the communications in this relationship.

Type of relationship: _____

Things that bug me: _____
_____
_____
_____
_____

How have I contributed to this communication gap?
_____
_____
_____
_____
_____
_____
_____

Guidelines I can use: _____
_____
_____
_____
_____
_____
_____
_____

Chapter 11 Relationships

Exercise 3

List all those people you wish to acknowledge and show appreciation. Make a note by each name indicating how you intend to show appreciation to these special people.

Person	Intention
Carla, my best friend	Tell her how I value her friendship

Chapter 11   Relationships

Exercise 4

To strengthen your understanding of different cultures, fill out the following list, noting similarities to and differences from your background. Feel free to add to the list and also jot notes at the bottom about different groups you would like to learn more about.

People That Are: **Things That Are:**

	The Same	Different
Chinese-American	_____	_____
African-American	_____	_____
Japanese-American	_____	_____
Irish-American	_____	_____
Native American	_____	_____
Mexican-American	_____	_____
Russian-American	_____	_____
Jewish	_____	_____

Chapter 11 Relationships

Exercise 5

Looking at the list in Exercise 4 I have placed a check mark next to the people I know the least about. I plan to learn more by:

1.

2.

3.

4.

5.

Case Study 1

Jahmal's Girl Trouble

Jahmal is having trouble explaining to his girlfriend how important school is to him and his future. For the last three nights she has called at nine o'clock and wanted him to take her to a club across town. As he explains to her again that he had to study for a big test scheduled for Friday, she gets angry and begins calling him names. After two minutes of listening to her calmly, he finds himself shouting back into the phone that she is nothing but a baby who wants her own way and that he is sick of her demands. Upon hanging up on her, he feels better for about two minutes but then realizes that she still doesn't understand how he feels.

1. How can Jahmal communicate more effectively?

2. What does he need to think of in terms of the healthiness of this relationship?

Case Study 2

Barbara Is Starting Over

Barbara is in her mid-forties and has just started school. She feels a great deal of pressure to succeed since she has three teenagers to raise on her own. She has not attended school in twenty years and has never worked outside the home. Her husband left her for a much younger co-worker and her friends are implying it's partially her fault for gaining weight and spending too much time on the kids' activities. Barbara believes that they are probably right and goes over and over what she should have done differently. As she starts school, all the classes seem to be moving too fast, but she doesn't want to appear stupid so she just sits in the back and hopes to catch up. As she works on her homework at night, she finds her mind drifting to the life she used to have and feels so guilty for what she believes to be her mistakes she has trouble concentrating. After she receives her first set of grades, she shuts herself in her bedroom and cries for two hours.

1. What changes does Barbara need to make in her relationship with herself to be successful?

Suggested Resource Material

Books: Additional Resources

Bach, Dr. George R., & Wyden, Peter. *The Intimate Enemy: How to Fight Fair in Love & Marriage.* Avon Publishing Co., 1976.

Norwood, Robin. *Women Who Love Too Much.* Recommended for both Men & Women. St. Martin's Press, 1985.

Cowan, Dr. Connell, & Kinder, Dr. Melvyn. *Smart Women/Foolish Choices.* NAL-Dutton Publishing Co., 1986.

Dowling, Colette. *The Cinderella Complex: Woman's Fear of Independence.* Pocket Books Publishing Co., 1990.

Smith, Manuel J. *When I Say No I Feel Guilty.* Bantam Books Publishing Co., 1985.

Forward, Dr. Susan, & Buck, Craig. *Toxic Parents: Overcoming Their Hurtful Legacy & Reclaiming Your Life.* Bantam Books Publishing Co., 1990.

Whitfield, Charles L., M.D. *Healing the Child Within: Discovery & Recovery for Adult Children of Dysfunctional Families.* Health Communications, 1987.

Gelles, Richard, & Straws, Murray. *Intimate Violence.* Simon & Schuster Publishing Co., 1989.

Buscaglia, Leo. *Love.* Fawcett Publishing Co., 1985.

Bass, Ellen, & Davis, Laura. *The Courage to Heal: A Guide for Women Survivors of Child Sexual Abuse.* Harper & Collins Publishing Co., 1988.

Goldberg, Herb, Ph.D. *The Hazard of Being Male.* Signet Publishing Co., 1977.

Burns, David M., M.D. *Intimate Connections.* NAL-Dutton Publishing Co., 1985.

Colgrove, Melba, Ph.D., Bloomfield, Harold H., M.D., & McWilliams, Peter. *How to Survive the Loss of a Love.* Bantam Publishing Co., 1984.

Diamond, Jed, L.C.S.W. *Looking for Love in All the Wrong Places.* Avon Publishing Co., 1989.

Chapter 12
Burnout and Self-Motivation

"I view each day as an exciting adventure that will make me richer through lessons I learn, the friends I make, and the progress toward my goals."

Personal Comment Sheet

Entry Date _____

Five self-positives:

1. _____

2. _____

3. _____

4. _____

5. _____

Getting Focused

How do I think the information I am about to read will help me reach my goals?

_____
_____
_____
_____
_____
_____

Since you first opened this book, you have learned a lot about yourself and what it takes to be successful. You should be proud of the steps you have taken to improve yourself and your life. But there is still a little more work to be done, a little more information to be shared.

Why did we save the topics Burnout and Self-Motivation for the last chapter? — because one can place a big hurdle across your road to success and the other gives you the strength to handle anything thrown your way.

Burnout

Figure 12-1

Most students suffer burnout at one time or another.

Burnout is a problem that will happen at one time or another to most students. You may only experience it for one day, or it may be serious enough that you think about dropping out of school. Burnout can affect anyone, but those most vulnerable to it are the ones who are trying the hardest to succeed. One of the causes of burnout is trying too hard and expecting too much from your efforts.

You have taken a big step toward a better life by getting an education, but you must realize that just because you start school, life will not get better for you overnight. Actually for a while it will get more complicated, because of the time and effort school will require on top of your other responsibilities. You will not see the fruits of your labor until you graduate and get a job. For some, this will be hard to accept. During your first series of classes you will enjoy the change of being in school, meeting new people, feeling some success, and the pride of telling your friends you are in college. It is during this time that you must prepare for the change in attitude (burnout) that you may experience some time in your life.

Signs of Burnout

Bob's hands shake as he tears open the envelope containing his second semester grades. Ignoring the two B grades, he begins yelling that his instructors don't understand how hard it is to go to school and hold a full-time job. His wife, Dorenda, tries to point out that C's show he did average work, which is nothing to be ashamed of. While she is talking, he gets even madder and tears

Creating Your Own Success

up his grade report. Storming off to their bedroom, he climbs into bed and draws the covers over his head. Concerned, Dorenda pulls out the article about burnout that she had just started reading when Bob exploded.

Reading over the warning signs, she spots several that Bob is suffering from. Just like the woman in the article, Bob is tired all of the time and complains about being overworked and under too much stress. Having just witnessed his short temper, she puts a check mark next to this symptom. Reading about how the woman in the article did not want to be around people or get out of bed, Dorenda lets out a sigh and looks over her shoulder into their bedroom, where Bob remains under the covers. Dorenda continues to scan the article, and notices that two more signs of burnout are an "I don't care" attitude and depression. Realizing that in a past job she experienced some of these same symptoms, she eagerly reads on about how to overcome burnout.

Tips to Overcoming Burnout

If, like Bob, you are experiencing burnout, the good news is that there are ways to overcome it. But what if you are like Dorenda and have suffered burnout in the past? By following these tips you can prevent burnout in the future.

Listen to yourself The first thing you need to do is get into the habit of listening to yourself. Unfortunately many of us have gotten into the habit of ignoring our positive inner voice. For example, if you hear a little voice saying "You don't have time to party tonight," you need to pay attention. This is your way of trying not to overload yourself.

Vary Your Routine Varying your routine through hobbies and outside interests helps to add balance to your life. When you enjoy a wide variety of activities, rather than just focusing on one, you lessen your chances of suffering from stress and burnout. If you have been reading all day then, for evening fun, pick an activity that involves another part of your brain — for example, go to a movie.

Visualize Your Goals When you visualize what your life will be like once you reach a goal, be sure your visualization is realistic. Remember that burnout happens when your visualization differs greatly from reality. A good example of this is the woman who says, "I'll be happy when I get married," and then spends all of her time reading romance novels and dreaming about her perfect mate. Because what she has visualized is so far from the reality of even the most perfect relationship, once she does get married burnout is almost assured because her marriage can never match up to her dreams. This will cause frustration and resentment, which are not the best ingredients for a happy long-term marriage.

Review Your Goals   Make it a habit to review your short-term goals once a week and long-term goals at least twice a year to make sure they still work for you. If they don't, then make changes so they are more in line with your present needs. Also, if you notice a loss of energy, which is one of the first signs of burnout, DON'T push harder. Most burnout victims, when they first notice a lack of energy, try even harder, work longer, and are more intense about reaching their goals. All of this extra effort just speeds up the burnout process. Instead, if this happens to you, just accept that your energy level is down. Work at your regular pace, and remind yourself that feeling tired won't last forever.

Remain Close to Others   When your stress level increases, it is important to remain close to yourself and other people. Spend time with just you and listen to yourself. Don't waste this time by distracting yourself with the TV or radio. Also, spend time with family and friends; this will help you remain close to them and fight any feelings of detachment you may be experiencing. Make sure that the family members and friends you choose to spend time with are positive and supportive in helping you reach your goals.

Treat Yourself   Treat yourself on a regular basis to something you enjoy and make it a habit to look at all of the progress you have made and not just how far you have to go.

Burnout Traps

There are burnout traps that you need to be sure you don't fall into. These are things that may make you feel better over the short-term, but actually only increase your problem, sometimes dramatically. These false cures are alcohol; drugs, both prescription and illegal; sex; gambling; or any activity that puts you at serious risk, such as driving at excessive speeds or taking unnecessary chances in relationships. All of these things may make you feel more alive in the short-run and may make you feel as if you have cured your burnout problem. In reality, this behavior is only speeding up and compounding the burnout process. For example, if the pressure of school is really getting to you and you have trouble relaxing at night, you might find that having a drink during the evening helps you relax and go to sleep. Pretty soon, as the pressure builds and your body gets use to one drink, it may take two to have the same effect, then three, and before you know it you are drinking all night. This example could be carried on even further (drinking during the day, loss of job, kicked out of school, etc.). Even in its mildest form it shows how these methods of handling stress and burnout don't work, because now you not only have burnout to deal with, but a drinking problem in addition.

Self-Motivation

Let's face it, sometimes it's not easy to keep yourself motivated. There are times when it seems like everyone and everything around you is trying to de-motivate you. Self-motivation takes effort and constructive inner dialogue, and it *can* be done, because the world is full of people who have mastered the art of keeping themselves motivated. These people aren't of a different species; they are just like you and me. How do we know they are just like you and me? Read their stories. One broadcaster was fired eighteen times in thirty years. Once she was out of work for almost a year, but she never gave up. Who is she? — successful radio and TV talk show personality Sally Jessy Raphael. A fifty-eight-year-old Indiana farm products salesman tried to come up with a better popcorn. But once he finally succeeded, nobody wanted to buy it because it cost more. Should he have listened to all of these negative voices and given up? Orville Redenbacher, who makes the best-selling popcorn in the world, is probably thankful he didn't. What writer lived in a trailer and worked at a laundry for sixty dollars a week and wrote three novels, all of which got rejected? Bet Stephen King is glad he didn't give up on himself. Look at the successful people around you. Study what makes them tick.

Some interesting observations about highly motivated people: You never find these people judging others or minding other people's business. They really believe that there is always more than one way to do things. Self-motivated people truly understand the saying, "God grant me the serenity to accept the things I cannot change, the courage to change the things I can, and the wisdom to know the difference." One of the secrets they have discovered is how to view the world as it really is, and not as they want it to be.

- Some people look at a glass of water and see it as being half full, while others look at the same glass of water and see it as half empty.
- Some people see retirement as the end, while others see it as a beginning.
- Some people see life as a blessing; others see life as a curse. It's all in how you look at it.

What are some of the things these highly motivated people do to keep themselves motivated? They really are not complicated, but they do require practice.

Suggestions for Keeping Yourself Motivated

Tricia is the single parent of two young children. To help support her family while going to school, she works as a cook three nights a week and cleans the houses of two elderly women on the weekends. While others might find this work demeaning, she takes pride in the service she provides and the money she can bring home to her family. After school at least three days a week, she puts the kids in the stroller and walks them to the park as part of her exercise program. Every night before she goes to sleep, she goes over her goals and positive self-talk statements. If, during these talks with herself, she catches worries trying to sneak in, she counteracts them by concentrating on how much she has already accomplished. Though life is hectic for her now, Tricia finds herself laughing more and feeling better about herself than ever before. Can you spot the positive action Tricia is taking that helps her feel this way?

Be Good to Yourself You can help achieve this by eating properly, exercising regularly, and getting plenty of rest. Set a high value on yourself. For example, if you owned a $1,000 pedigreed show dog would you keep it up all night, feed it junk food, and never let it out of its pen? Probably not. Well, aren't you just as valuable? Feeling good is a definite plus in keeping yourself motivated.

Figure 12-2

Be good to yourself by exercising regularly.

Concentrate on Now Stop worrying about things that haven't happened yet. Concentrate on what's happening now. Take it one day at a time. A simple example of this is the student who is required to reach a typing speed of 70 wpm (words per minute). He has several months to reach this speed. However, with a typing speed of 15 wpm after just one week of classes, he is convinced he will never type 70 wpm, "NO WAY." Just a week ago he didn't even know how to turn the typewriter on and had never typed before. After only one week he had achieved a gain of 15 wpm. Another example of this is the student who just knows she is going to fail Accounting II, when she hasn't even taken Accounting I yet. Concentrate on what you have achieved, and what you are doing right now, not what may or may not happen months from now.

Creating Your Own Success

Let Go Accept what you can't change and let it go. Have you ever noticed you're never unhappy or depressed over something until you find out about it? The event may have taken place hours, days, or even weeks ago, but even though it is past and there is nothing you can do about it you allow it to depress or upset you. This is not to suggest that you should be heartless. But, if you cannot change it and your being depressed and feeling unhappy won't make a difference, then just accept it and let it go. For example, you start your day off feeling great, you take extra care in dressing, and everything is just wonderful. You feel good, look good, and it turns out to be a fantastic day. Everything goes like clockwork all day long. You make a big sale or you really impress the teacher with your speech. It just couldn't have been a better day. It's almost time to go home and, glancing in a mirror, you notice a big piece of spinach is stuck between your two front teeth. Now until that moment you didn't know about it and you were feeling terrific. You start wondering "How long has it been there? Who else noticed it?" Before you know it, you have convinced yourself you are a tacky useless scumbag, and your whole perfect day is ruined. But, until you found out about it, everything was fine. You can't undo or change what has happened, and probably no one else paid much attention to it or even cared if they did. If you let a small thing like this make you unhappy, imagine how you make yourself feel over bigger things. If you can't change it, then accept it and let it go.

Keep Things in Perspective Ask yourself, how important is this? Keep things in perspective. Few things in life are absolutely perfect, and yet they are useful and good. For example, one of your assignments is to complete a map of the United States for a Travel and Tourism class. You have entered the states' names on at least 20 maps, but each time you are unhappy with your handwriting. You have stressed yourself out over this map for hours trying to make it perfect; yet the whole purpose of the map was to see if you knew the correct locations of the states, NOT your lettering ability. It doesn't have to be perfect. Another example of this is the baker who threw out all the biscuits that didn't rise as high or got a little browner than the rest. All the biscuits tasted the same and were delicious, but the baker spent hours trying to make all the biscuits the same, perfect. Always try to do your best, but don't whip yourself every time your best is not perfect.

Stop De-Motivators Learn to spot the de-motivators and stop them. De-motivators can be people or things. If you know someone who is always looking at the down side of everything, make sure you don't allow them to affect your mood. These are the people who always seem to be having a rotten day, the ones who never seem to have any luck. They are always down on the world and everyone in it. When you meet people like this and you know there is nothing you can say or do that will help them, then tell yourself "I really don't need this right now," and spend as little time with them as possible.

Also, don't let other people use you and then hate yourself for letting them do so. You're not doing them any favors in the long run when you do their work for them. If you continue doing it, then you are training them to expect it, and believe me they will. Let them tend their own gardens, and you tend yours. They will respect you more and you will respect yourself more.

Let go of all the unnecessary things in your life that stress you and de-motivate you. Examples might be:

A. Your ride never picks you up on time and you're always late.
    FIND ANOTHER RIDE.
B. You can't study at home because of all the noise.
    STUDY AT THE LIBRARY.
C. You are in an abusive relationship.
    CALL A SHELTER AND GET HELP.

Don't Fear Failure Don't let fear of failure be a de-motivator. Do what you fear the most and you control fear. For example, the first time you have to give a speech, you may have nightmares about all the things that could happen, including scenes where you forget your speech, your dress falls off, your fly is open, or you shake so badly you can't speak. You can't get out of the speech, so you take a deep breath, get up there, and give it your best shot. Surprise! You feel more confident now that you have survived and learned from this experience. You will probably always be a little nervous every time, but you will never again feel that overwhelming fear that you felt the first time.

Look at the Positive Look at the positive side of things first, instead of the negative. Sometimes you may have to give yourself a good talking to. If you find there are times when you have this irritating little self-talk voice inside that always wants to be negative, then give that little voice a name. It can be any name you choose, like Pesky. Tell Pesky to get lost because you're in charge.

Learn to tell the difference between your positive self-talk and your negative self-talk. Not all your voices are negative; sometimes you need to listen when the voice is trying to keep you from doing something you will regret. It may be your better judgment talking to you.

Laugh Having a good sense of humor will help you to stay motivated. Don't take yourself or what others say too seriously. There is humor in almost everything in life. Lighten up and learn to laugh at yourself too.

Choose Your Experience Sometimes you have to let go, and go with the flow. There will be times in your life when you will have to let go of having control. For example, Mike and Larry both get off at noon on Fridays. Both need to go to the license bureau. They both arrive at 1:00 p.m. The license bureau is full and there are very long lines. Mike is upset at how long the lines are and starts shifting from one foot to the other. He starts changing lines, trying to move everyone faster. He is really getting angry because he feels they should have more help. These people are so stupid not bringing everything they need and making everyone wait. He reaches the window and he doesn't have his tax slip so he must wait while they check his taxes through the computer. When he leaves the license bureau at 1:45 p.m., he is grouchy, irritable, and has a headache.

Larry realizes there is nothing he can do about the long wait. He just relaxes and moves with the line. He smiles and talks to the other people. He notices a little boy sitting by the window reading a book. The little boy was there when he came in; he smiles to himself thinking how patiently that little boy waits for his parent, while the man in the other line is having a fit. Larry thinks about the upcoming weekend. He is going to the lake to ski, swim, and just have fun. It is 100 degrees outside and he is sure glad the bureau is air-conditioned and cool. Larry leaves the license bureau at 1:45 p.m., smiling and whistling.

Larry understood that by controlling his emotions he could choose the experience he would have waiting in line even though he could not control the situation. What can you learn from these two examples?

A Few of the Secrets of Life

If we were walking along a sandy beach and stumbled across a magic bottle, we would ask the genie inside to let us meet each of you. We wish we could see your face, know your name, hear your story. We wish we could sit with you and, using every ounce of strength we have, give you a final verbal push onto your personal road to success. But without that magic genie, we have had to depend on our words to reach out to you, to touch your mind and heart. As you cover the miles on your road to success, if you feel yourself stumbling, whether it is next week or ten years from now, we hope you will open this book again and find within its pages the words that will give you the strength and courage to go on. A good place to start is with the following secrets of life. As you travel on your own success journey, add to this list the secrets that your experiences teach you. Then, as you taste success and personal achievement, pass along what you have learned to others who are struggling to get started just like you are now. And most of all keep learning, keep growing, and NEVER GIVE UP.

- Know the difference between worrying and forming a realistic plan of action. Worrying about a problem will accomplish nothing, whereas a realistic plan of action will direct your energy, allowing you to work your way out of the problem.

- Spend no more than two minutes a day thinking about what "could have been" or "should have been." Instead, accept things as they are and keep your eyes focused on your goals.

- Remember that everyone is scared some of the time. The whole key is to keep your mind busy with productive activity so that it doesn't have time to be scared.

- Think and act positively, ignoring the little voice in your head that whispers "you're a failure" and any number of other hateful things. Drown that little voice with positive messages, messages that when thought of often enough and long enough will become true.

- Accept that you and you alone can make your life what you want it to be. It is the one thing, the only thing, you totally own and each day of it you are given a chance to use the time wisely or waste it in self-pity.

- Each experience life gives us offers a lesson if we are willing to search ourselves for its meaning. Sometimes it takes years for the lesson to become evident to us, but it is ALWAYS there.

- Forget the word "fair." When you are born, God does not send along a certificate guaranteeing that life will treat you fairly. Time spent wishing for fairness or griping that life is not fair is the ultimate waste of time.

- You can learn by doing. As we've said all along, successful people practice success. Don't expect your first attempts to be perfect and don't allow yourself to quit. In time you will gain in both skill and confidence.

- It takes as much energy to be miserable as it does to be happy.

- This is your life, the only one you will have on this earth — so take control.

- At the end of every day, right before you go to sleep, think about one good thing you accomplished that day and one thing you are thankful for.

Use this space to add your own secrets of life.

Chapter 12

More Steps On My Road To Success
A Personal Review

1. What were the key concepts discussed about burnout and self-motivation?

2. How do I plan to put this new burnout and self-motivation knowledge into effect?

3. What are the areas I don't understand or need more information on?

4. What is my game plan for getting the additional information I need?

5. What positive changes do I see in myself?

Chapter 12 Burnout and Self-Motivation

Exercise 1

To help myself stay motivated I am going to:

1. Be good to myself by

2. Stop worrying about

3. Get rid of the following de-motivators in my life

4. I am going to get rid of these de-motivators by

Chapter 12   Burnout and Self-Motivation

Exercise 2

Make a list of all the special ways you keep yourself motivated. Give your list a title; for example, "Put Me In, Coach," "My Booster Shot List," or "What Works for Me." Add to it every time you find something that works for you. Keep this list handy and review it often. You may even want to share it with others.

Chapter 12   Burnout and Self-Motivation

Exercise 3

Since burnout and stress often go hand in hand, let's take a look at what events cause you to feel stress.

MY STRESS BUTTONS:

1. _____
2. _____
3. _____
4. _____

NOW LOOK AT EACH ITEM LISTED IN ONE OF TWO WAYS:

1. Ways I can learn to relieve the stress buttons I listed

2. Ways I can program my brain so that these stress buttons become positive for me

Chapter 12 Burnout and Self-Motivation

Exercise 4

1. Write down all the situations in which you have experienced burnout and how you handled your feelings. Be prepared to discuss in class what you learned from this experience.

2. During the class discussion, enter ways your classmates dealt with burnout that you had not thought of for future reference.

Chapter 12 Burnout and Self-Motivation

Exercise 5

My Life Philosophy

This class is almost over. During it you have made new friends with whom you have discussed many ways to be successful. Keeping in mind all that you have learned, write down in less than three sentences the main ideals you plan to live your life by.

_____

_____

_____

I have finished this class through my own hard work and effort, of which I am proud. I am also proud because I have made or have started to make the following changes in me.

_____

_____

_____

My promise: If and when I begin to feel doubt lurking around me, I will pull out this sheet and remind myself of all the power for success that flows through me.

Name: _____ Date: _____

Case Study

Accentuate the Positive — Eliminate the Negative

Lesia has been going to school for three months and, though at first she enjoyed it, now each morning it is harder to get up. As she drags around the house getting ready, she finishes her third cup of coffee and fourth cigarette. Looking into her closet she finds that all that is clean are her "fat clothes," those that make her feel like a two-ton truck. Leaving the house 15 minutes late, she hurries to the bus stop only to see the bus pulling out from the curb. She studies her bus schedule and sees that another one will be along in 35 minutes. As she starts to pull out her English book to review for a test that afternoon, a girlfriend she hasn't seen for years sits down next to her. Kaleen begins chatting about not being able to find a job and how unfair that old biddy Mrs. Hernandez is down at the employment office. Before Lesia knows what has happened, she too is complaining about how unfair life is and the two decide to go shopping to cheer themselves up.

1. How could Lesia have planned her morning so that her day had a better start?

2. What happened to Lesia's motivation when Kaleen sat down?

3. What steps should Lesia take to get herself back on track with her goals?

4. What steps could she take to encourage Kaleen to change her attitude?

Creating Your Own Success

Suggested Resource Material

Books: Additional Resources

Dyer, Dr. Wayne. *Pulling Your Own Strings.* Avon Publishing Co., 1979.

Freldenberger, Dr. Herbert J., & North, Gail. *Burnout—How to Spot It, How to Reverse It, & How to Prevent It.* Viking Penguin Publishing Co., 1990.

Hill, Napoleon. *Think & Grow Rich.* Fawcett Publishing Co., 1987.

James, Muriel. *Born to Win.* Addison-Wesley Publishing Co., 1990.

Use this page for motivational swaps.
Sayings that I will use to help motivate myself.

Use this page for motivational swaps.
Sayings that I will use to help motivate myself.

Index

A
abuse, drug and alcohol, 179–196
    learning to say no, 182–187
    reasons for, 181–182
    toward recovery, 188–190
appearance, 165–172
    checklist, 174
    clothing, 169–172
    first impression, 165–167
    guidelines, 167–172
    self, 167–169
attendance, x
attitudes, 73–84
    improvement, 79–82, 83, 84
    negative, 74–75, 76–77
    positive, 75–76, 77, 85

B
body language, 162–165
    defined, 162–163
    messages, 163–165
book, parts of a, 56–57
    appendix, 57
    bibliography, 57
    chapters or lessons, 57
    glossary, 57
    index, 57
    preface or introduction, 56
    table of contents, 56
burnout, 218–220
    overcoming, 219–220, 232
    signs of, 218–219, 231
    traps, 220

C
campus resources, 10–11
    academic dean/ registrar, 10
    employment assistance, 11
    financial aid, 11
    other, 11
    school catalog or bulletin, 10
    school organizations, 11
    student services, 10
    tutoring, 11
case study, 18, 37, 52, 71, 93, 120, 139, 158–159, 176–177, 195, 213, 214, 234

E
eye contact, 8, 43

G
getting acquainted, 4–5, 7–10
    classmates, 4–5
    instructor, 4
goals, 21–31
    achievement, 28–31
    action plan, 26–28, 36
    failure, 28–29
    goal busters, 22–23
    steps to achieve, 22
    types, 23–26
        intermediate, 25, 34
        long-term, 24, 33
        short-term, 25–26, 35

H
human relations, guidelines, 77–79

L
listening, 40–44
    effective techniques, 50–51
        ask questions, 43
        listen actively, 43
        listen smart, 45
        listen to more than just words, 42
        listen with more than just your ears, 43
    stumbling blocks to, 46–47, 49–50
        closed-mindedness, 41
        daydreaming, 41
        false attention, 41
        hard-to-understand subjects, 41
        memorizing, 41–42
        personality listening, 42

M
memory, 123–130
    long-term, 124
    short-term, 124
    techniques, 125–130, 132, 133–134, 135, 136, 137

O

outline
  listening, 49–51
  reading and taking notes, 67–68

R

reading, 56–60
  effective, 57–58, 66
    steps in:
      ask help from others, 60
      decide what is important, 59
      prepare physically, 59
      prepare mentally, 58–62
      preview the chapter, 59
      review what you read, 60
      study further, 60
  practice, 69
  types of, 57–58

relationships, 200–206
  appreciation, 204–205, 210
  change, 203–204, 214
  communication in, 200–203, 213
  dysfunctional, 205
  harassment, 206

S

self-motivation, maintaining, 221–225, 229, 230
substance abuse, 179–190
  avoidance, 182–187
  discovery, 187–188
  reasons for, 181–182
  recovery, 188–190
success, 75, 85

T

taking notes, 61–65, 66
  format, 64
  from the textbook, 63–65
    developing an outline, 63
    summarizing, 63
  in the classroom, 62–63
  key words, 62
  searching for clues, 62–63
  practice, 70
  reasons for:
    better understanding, 62
    easy review, 62
    effective use of time, 61
    improved listening, 61
    positive attitude, 61
test-taking, 141–151
  guidelines, 145–146
  preparation, 142–145, 153–154
  strategy, 146–151, 156–157
time management, 95–106
  basic principles, 96–101
  tools, 102–106, 108–115, 116, 117, 118, 121